A TALE OF AN ORDINARY
LIFE CALLED TO DO THE
EXTRAORDINARY

Peter's Song

ROBERT HAWKES

Ark House Press
PO Box 1722, Port Orchard, WA 98366 USA
PO Box 1321, Mona Vale NSW 1660 Australia
PO Box 318 334, West Harbour, Auckland 0661 New Zealand
arkhousepress.com

Cataloguing in Publication Data:
Title: Peter's Song
ISBN: 9780648263968 (pbk.)
Subjects: Fiction; Christian;
Other Authors/Contributors: Hawkes, Robert

Design by initiateagency.com

For my family,
for all the love
and all the laughter
we share.

CONTENTS

INTRODUCTION

A little over two thousand years ago there was a man called Simon Bar Jonah who lived in a small town to the north of the Sea of Galilee in northern Israel. No one today really knows what he looked like, but assumptions have been made about his physique based on his ethnicity and the likely diet of his day. No doubt he would have been physically strong, as any fisherman throughout the ages has had to be, and he would have been accustomed to working hard to earn a living pulling fish from the depths of the sea. His hands would have been rough from the manual labour of rowing, working with wet nets and handling coarse ropes. He would have carried with him the characteristic odour of his trade, acquired by cleaning and selling whatever he caught, but in the context of all the other aromas of his day, which we have now become so sensitised to, it would not necessarily have been considered particularly unpleasant or unusual, just distinctive of his trade.

By modern standards, Simon would probably be regarded as poorly educated. He would have spoken with a distinctive regional accent and with a vernacular that on occasions betrayed his lack of learning and his Galilean roots. He might reasonably have expected to live out the normal life of a 1st century fisherman, assuming his health permitted it, in much the same way as his ancestors and neighbours would have done.

On one occasion whilst out fishing, he was addressed by an itinerant preacher who started calling him by a different name: Peter, (or Cephas in his own language) indicating a particular calling on his life which would take him far beyond the hills that surrounded his home, family and his everyday working life on the water. This itinerant preacher who we know as Jesus of Nazareth, told him to leave everything behind and follow him. The name Peter, which Jesus gave him means 'rock' and implies a sturdy, solid, reliable, dependable character, which Jesus discerned in him even though many of the early accounts written about Peter by his contemporaries would suggest otherwise. Notwithstanding his numerous misunderstandings and failings, Jesus chose Simon Bar Jonah as the man he wanted to build his church on.

The less than reliable traits exhibited by Peter, which are recorded in the Gospels, suggest a transformation had to take place in Peter for Jesus to be able to fulfil this expectation. This simple fisherman would have been more at home spending his days in an old wooden fishing boat, with all the associated detritus of his profession slopping about his feet in fetid puddles at the bottom of his boat, than taking a leading role in any world changing movement. But he was chosen by Jesus to be one of his key ambassadors, to continue his unique work after his death, ultimately changing the history of the world. The transformation from the unassuming fisherman into an apostle, from the impulsive man portrayed in the Gospels to the great apostle in the Book of Acts, who is now venerated around the world, is a remarkable one. My intention with this work of fiction is not to add to scripture, or even expound on it necessarily, but to wonder at the personal battles that such a man would have had to go through in this transformation.

It has been my intention from the outset not to misrepresent or change any of the historical events recorded in the Bible, but just to add some colour around certain passages. The colour of everyday life, to try and break through what can sometimes feel like an impenetrable crust which has formed over these events with the passage of time. This is particularly true for those of us who live in the west, in the 21st century.

For us, trying to gain a better understanding of what Jesus said and did involves not only a journey back through two thousand years into another era, but also into another culture, utterly different from our own. It is my hope that this story helps to break through the impenetrable crust and sheds a little light beneath it.

Whilst writing this book I have been guilty of self-projection on to some of the characters, but I have done so to try and emphasise their ordinariness and their humanity. I hope that by so doing I have shown the extra-ordinariness and the new life which God wrought in them and through them by the empowering of His Holy Spirit poured out on these early believers.

I should also mention here, particularly because this book is based in the earliest days of the fledgling Christian church that I have endeavoured to avoid anything that hints at Gnosticism, or any of the other heretical distortions of the gospel that dogged the early church; however subtle, overt, or otherwise. I would also like to state here that the New Testament records various confrontations between Jesus and the religious leaders of his time, particularly the Chief Priests, Scribes and Pharisees, especially those who were responsible for the corrupt, temple system of its day. Reference is made to these confrontations and the lasting impressions they left on the believers as an illustration of the times in which they lived. Where I have made such references they should not be extrapolated into any statement about the Jewish people or their history prior to, or subsequent to these events. Jesus came first to the Jews. He was himself a Jew, as were his first followers.

It is my hope that this book will first and foremost entertain, but I also hope it will help anyone who feels the call to leave the familiar and comfortable and risk all to follow Jesus into the impossible, just as Simon Bar Jonah did.

SOME ARE BORN EQUAL,
OTHERS LESS SO.

Towards the end of the reign of King Herod the Great, the Bible tells us that Jesus was born to Joseph and Mary. A peasant couple from a small hill town in Galilee in the north of Israel. Joseph was a Tecton, a labourer, more traditionally regarded as a carpenter and the expectation was that his son, when he was old enough, would learn his father's trade and help provide for the family until he himself married, raised a family and repeated the cycle of life, raising up sons to help him with his work and daughters to help their mother with her work, until they in turn married and so on, ad infinitum.

There are a few accounts of the birth of Jesus. Some are more reliable than others, but as history shows there was something extraordinary about these peasants' son. It would appear that he dutifully learnt carpentry and became known to some as 'that carpenter from Nazareth', but his destiny ultimately lay elsewhere and the irrelevant, insignificant hilltop village of Nazareth gained significance and notoriety as the home of the man who changed the world forever. Though Joseph, Mary and Jesus were known to come from Nazareth, the most widely accepted version of Jesus' birth has it happening in Bethlehem, some seventy miles south of Nazareth as the crow flies (considerably further as the donkey walks).

He was born in a stable among livestock. The animals' feed trough was adapted to be used as his crib. Even as peasant births go, his was a humble start. The stable was most likely fashioned from one of the small caves that dot the Judean hills around Bethlehem. It would have been dirty and would have smelled strongly of the animal waste that made up the largest proportion of the damp floor, which the new parents now knelt upon, their knees darkened by the liquid seeping into the divots they made as they knelt to peer at their first born. Parts of the roof and walls of the cave would have been blackened by soot from decades, if not centuries of oil lamps, torches and small fires lit by the shepherds tending their flocks of sheep and goats that grazed the hillsides. The darkened interior did nothing to reflect the meagre light emitted by their solitary oil lamp, so Joseph had to hold it aloft over the baby as he slept so they could make out his beautiful features, marvelling at how handsome he was, as every parent does. Revelling in the most ordinary murmur, flicker of an eyelid or twitch of a tiny finger.

This baby's humble surroundings were about as ordinary as this birth got. When shepherds arrived outside the stable saying that angelic beings had told them about the baby, shortly followed by some far eastern nobility bearing gifts for their son their newfound parenthood took on a significance far beyond that normally experienced by first time parents. Even when taking the baby up to the temple in Jerusalem to present him before the Lord, as every law abiding Jew was required to do, the prophets there uttered such incredible things over the boy that the parents were left speechless. To be fair neither parent could have been more proud than they already were. They had a son and that gift affirmed both of them as being blessed by God. Particularly Mary.

Herod was a conniving, paranoid and vicious king. The palaces he built for himself were always designed with an easy escape route for himself, should they be attacked. Tremendous effort and resources were spent constructing these residences so that just in case the unimaginable should happen and the palace was attacked without warning, he at least would be safe. So, when the nobility from the east had made their curtesy visit to the sovereign, they had unwittingly alerted him to the birth of the boy they believed would become the greatest king of all time. The paranoid Herod did not share their joy and even though he evidently did not have many years left in him, he decided to eradicate any potential future threat to his throne the only way he knew. He had no way of identifying this child himself, but he knew enough: he was born in Bethlehem, just six miles to the south and the child was a new-born boy. Orders were given and soldiers despatched to Bethlehem to annihilate a generation of new-born boys under the age of two years. A simple, brutal plan which would have achieved its objectives had the baby's parents not been prompted to flee the region by an angelic visitation, thereby preserving their baby's life.

Around the time of Jesus's birth, a son was born to the wife of a fisherman called Jonah who lived in Bethsaida, a small town on the northern shores of the Sea of Galilee, just east of Capernaum. Though born around the same time as Jesus, this child was not in the same immediate danger from the murderous ravings of his paranoid King that his peers were some sixty miles to the south. The child's passage into this world was nonetheless as precarious as any other child's at that time. If he did survive the immediate dangers of the birth, in the primitive house with the mud or dung plastered walls and the thatched roof of mud and reeds above his naked and vulnerable body, he would only have a 50:50 chance of surviving childhood. His mother would probably have been attended and assisted throughout the birth by the hands of the wiser older women who lived in the community. And as with the boy Jesus, it would have been expected that this boy, whose father gave him the name Simon, would learn the skills of his father's trade as soon as he was old enough and help him with the business of catching fish on the Sea of Galilee. In the same way that his father Jonah would have done with his father before him. There was no higher calling, no greater expectation than to live this simple cycle of life, and in any case, if he could catch fish, he and his family would never go hungry. It was both a humble but respected calling which would bring a certain honour to his family and particularly to his father who would have been considered to have brought up a good son, not a foolish boy.

There is no record of Jonah or his wife receiving any angelic visitation foretelling them of any great things their son would become known for. However, there are records of the boy's adult life and there are eyewitness accounts of some of the wonderful things he did, the things he said and was a party to. But he will always be remembered for being the rough, earnest, humble fisherman from Galilee who very publically struggled to grasp the meaning of what Jesus taught him. A man who seemed to pioneer the art of failing and weakness for billions of us who would follow in his footsteps, allowing his God to show the world through him, His gracious, redemptive nature expressed in and through such an ordinary life.

About six or seven years prior to these two births, in the city of Jerusalem another poor family, whose names have never been recorded in the annals of history, had a son. Though some events surrounding the son are recorded. The father of this child would have prayed that the baby his young wife carried in her belly would be a boy. He would have projected similar expectations on to him as both Jonah and Joseph would later do with their male offspring. Simply that he would honour his father and mother, follow his father's trade and grow up to be a handsome young man, earning the respect of their neighbours who in turn would inevitably want to arrange for the most beautiful of their daughters to be betrothed to him.

On the night this boy was born his father waited anxiously just outside the house listening to his wife's laboured cries and drawn out grunts as she struggled to bring this new life into the world. When her cries eventually stopped they were replaced by the new-born's first gasped breaths, exhaled as short staccato cries, sounding somewhat weak and strangled compared to its mother's full blown unrestrained bellowing.

The relief the new father felt at the sound of the child was overwhelming and he wanted to go back into the house and see this new addition to their family, but protocol dictated that he wait until the women attending his wife had finished their work. As the two women exited the house to find him, neither looked him in the eye and neither told him whether it was a boy or a girl. His heart sank slightly and mouth grew dry. The child was obviously alive because he had heard it, so as his heart started to sink ever so slightly he assumed their furtiveness was because they knew how much he wanted a boy and they had delivered him a girl instead. They motioned for him to go into the back room; one of the women holding back the frayed drape that covered the doorway and the other making a sideways motion with her head. As he ducked his head under the drawn drape and passed between the women, the older one said, "God is faithful, my son," as she let the drape fall across the door behind him. This confused him as their manner and the troubled, exhausted face of his wife now before him said otherwise. He moved slowly to the bedside and looked at the tiny bundle she was nursing in her arms. She said nothing and turned her focus back to the baby and tried to encourage it to feed.

The father wanted to view the child, to see the glory of his hoped for son. As he moved to pull back the wrappings the mother moved her hand to prevent him, but he wanted to know whether he had a son or a daughter and gently swatted her hand aside insistently. She didn't protest but watched his face as he pulled back the blood spotted cloth to reveal their son's nakedness. She watched his surprised delight which caused both his eyebrows to rise as he discovered that he was indeed the father of a boy, fade then dissolve as its zenith, slowly receding to form the furrowed brow of a man trying to make sense out of the confusion his brain now wrestled with. As his eyes moved down from the severed umbilical and all-important genitals of the boy, he now took in the unusual shape of the boy's legs and feet. They weren't quite right. A new-born's limbs (not that he'd studied many), were usually drawn up and could appear curved, but not like these limbs. They were curved abnormally, inwards under the child's torso. The feet almost doubling back on the legs themselves. The feet ugly, red, fleshy lumps rather than the beautiful, perfect miniatures of what they should mature into. He looked around the room to see if there were any more lamps he could bring to the bed so he could get a better look. There weren't any and he realised this wasn't a trick of the poor light. His son was deformed. His confusion turned to deep sadness then resentment. His resentment turned to anger that needed expression as it so often did when his plans were frustrated. What did those old crones mean "God is faithful"? What had he done to deserve being treated like this by God...?

Rather than look at her husband the mother attended to her son, encouraging him to feed as if by pouring more of herself into him his legs would somehow miraculously fill out and straighten by themselves. Try as she might she could not ignore the despair in her own heart and that of her husband's. He turned to leave the room without speaking to her. She didn't want him to leave. This was their child, the moment she had hoped they would savour together. He flung the soiled cloth back over the child's nakedness and headed for the door. As he turned, she blurted, "What shall we call him?" breaking the silence that had filled the room since he had entered it. She tucked the cloth gently back around her baby to comfort him. The father stopped and exhaled an exasperated breath. It didn't matter what they called him. It wasn't going to change who, or rather what he was... even if he lived. Their neighbours and their neighbours' children would have names of their own for him. He'd seen it on so many occasions before and as a child himself he had teased those who'd carried abnormalities from birth or who'd been disfigured by disease or bones that hadn't healed properly after a break. The blind, the deaf, the lame and leprous were all shunned by society in a belief that it was God's judgement on the individual, or the individual's family for some hidden sin in their past.

"Mephibosheth," he said, without turning back. "Call him Mephibosheth."

This wasn't a family name that would traditionally have been bestowed on the child. The boy's father didn't want to dishonour one of his forefathers by passing on their name to this latest imperfect addition to the family line. Rather, knowing the history of Israel and the story of Jonathan's son of the same name who was crippled in an accident at the age of five. His nurse dropped him, as they fled following the news of the death of the boy's father and Grandfather in battle. That Mephibosheth of history was lame in both feet for the rest of his life as a consequence of being dropped. It seemed fitting on this night to adopt that name for his son. He then left the room for the darkness of the starless night outside and the darkness of his soul within.

The boy Jesus of Nazareth didn't meet Peter of Bethsaida until he was a man of about thirty years of age. Jesus never met Mephibosheth of Jerusalem in person, who contrary to his father's expectations did survive childhood, but he may have walked past him and the hordes of other beggars like him that were placed by the roadsides that led up to the temple in Jerusalem. It was hoped that passers-by, worshippers and God fearers alike, would have compassion on these unfortunates and condescend to drop a few prutah, or a piece of bread into their outstretched hands or begging bowls. When Mephibosheth was forty years old, Peter met him some three or four years after he had first met Jesus. This Mephibosheth's name is not actually recorded in history, but the meeting between him and Peter is. He was a beggar. The only career open to him, embarked upon out of necessity. As a young baby he looked frail and not expected to live past infancy, but he was a survivor. From a young age his mother would bring him up to the Gate Beautiful that led into the temple and would sit behind him displaying his disfigurement and bewailing her personal misfortune to try and attract the pity of passers-by.

When the boy grew older, he was dragged up to his usual spot on a cart pulled by his more able bodied siblings and sometimes by his Father, where he would be left to fend for himself. If he was successful he would eat. If by God's mercy he was particularly successful, the whole family would eat. However, success was far from certain. The wealthier religious elite would not trouble themselves with the plight of the common man. Much less one who bore the marks of being cursed by God, as these crippled beggars did. Their inured consciences remained untouched as they walked past in their flowing robes, heads held high, confident in their righteous standing before God, ignoring plaintive requests for scraps and coins. They did not look down except only to reassure themselves of the difference between their great and blessed standing and that of those evidently cursed. It helped them feel justified as they moved towards the inner courts of the temple confident in their own minds that God was ready to receive them. If they had stopped just once and deigned to just ask him his name, their consciences might have been pricked ever so slightly, as they could not help but be reminded of their beloved King David honouring Jonathan's crippled son.

Mephibosheth and all the other "Mephibosheths" would watch the worshippers enter the temple with some envy. The few passers-by that stopped to speak to them, especially those that dropped a coin or two in their hands, were watched on their way with the blessing of the poor beggars resting upon them, as they too moved up and into the magnificent temple gates where their God *was* ready to receive them with joy.

Eventually Mephibosheth became adopted into the family of harlots, drunkards and other social outcasts. They shared more in common with each other than they did with the rest of 'decent society'. These unloved, unwanted of society, more-sinned-against than sinners themselves, would go out of their way to share their bread with the perpetually hungry like Mephibosheth, just to make sure they were OK for another day. If one of the 'piously superior' was watching it was even more rewarding to share the little they had with the 'cursed of God' because it was a way of thumbing their noses at them and their form of religion, which attempted to stand on values more twisted than Mephibosheth's legs.

THURSDAY NIGHT AND SATURDAY MORNING

The first time she saw the friends of her father who'd come from the north to stay was a Thursday, before Passover. Lois thought they looked rough and unkempt and this worried her. They spoke funny too. They didn't sound the same as other men in the city and although they were much older than her four years of age, she thought it strange that they couldn't pronounce their words properly. Not all of them were scary. There was one of them who seemed really nice. He had a kindly disposition and smiled at her whenever he caught her looking at him. She liked him straight away because he made her feel special…

Lois's mother Esther and her father Ahaz spent a lot of time preparing for their guests' stay, making sure everything was just so. Moving furniture in to and out of the upper room of their home, and preparing food for their stay, a lot of food, and wine. When evening came and all the guests had assembled in the upper room for the meal, her mother and father stayed upstairs just inside the door waiting on the diners, ready to fetch anything they needed. The meal went on for a long time which annoyed her grandfather who remained in the ground floor room with her. A lot things annoyed her grandfather, but nothing more than when her parents were obliged to attend to others' needs rather than his own. And so it was on this night and particularly so whenever it was his duty to look after the youngest grandchild. However, not uncharacteristically, as this evening wore on the old man had fallen asleep after he'd eaten his meal and Lois had become bored. She loved her grandfather, but was wary of him when he became bad tempered like this. Anyway, as he'd fallen asleep she decided to let herself out of the house on the pretence of going to see if her mother needed any help. The truth was that she was curious about what the guests were doing upstairs, particularly the nice man who she hoped would make a fuss of her. She quietly lifted the latch and slipped out into the cool of the night. Turning left she walked quietly along the front of the house trailing her fingers along the rough stone wall and around the corner to the steps that led up the side of the building to the upper room. As she reached the foot of the steps the door at the top burst open and the warm yellow light of the interior spilled out in stark contrast with the deep dark blue of the Jerusalem night sky. One of the visitors hurried out and ran down the steps, momentarily startling her. She hugged the wall as he reached the bottom of the steps, suddenly feeling vulnerable and trying to become invisible, immediately regretting leaving the safety of the interior. The man briefly looked in her direction without really seeing her. He seemed distracted and was muttering something. Without pausing he stole away into the shadows of the streets that lead away from their house, momentarily glancing over his shoulder before disappearing into the dark.

The unexpected encounter scared Lois and she wanted to be with her parents now more than she did before. She tentatively started to ascend the steps, keeping a wary eye fixed on the sliver of light that escaped past the door which had been left ajar by the hurriedly departing figure. She didn't take her eyes off the door just in case another of the men came rushing out. When she reached the top of the steps she peered through the doorway. She could see her parents, just inside the door, ready to serve the men reclining at the table at the other end of the long room.

There were other women sat in the corner to her left. The far end of the room was brightly lit. She could see that the best lamps in the house had been brought up for the guests: the round lamps with the six spouts were set on the table. These gave out the best light and she could see the faces of the men on the far side of the table. Lois slipped silently around the door into the room and some of the women in the corner forced a smile at her. The men were all listening attentively to the nice man who was speaking gently to them, but what he was saying seemed to be making them sad. She couldn't understand what he was saying partly because of his strange accent, but also it was grown up stuff, which didn't really interest her, but it all struck her as odd.

She continued to watch silently from behind her parents for a while, not wanting to alert them to her presence in case they took her back downstairs again.

After he had finished speaking the nice man closed his eyes and started to sing. It was a sad song and the other men joined in, rather half-heartedly she thought; as if they weren't really enjoying the song. This was particularly true of the biggest man in the group who sat staring at the table in front of him, barely uttering a word. He looked the saddest, or maybe the angriest of them all. It was true, Peter did not like how the evening was developing and his heavy heart prevented him from singing the song that was well known to them all. Instead Peter sat sullenly, barely mouthing the words. His breath not able to give the song life.

"What are you doing up here, Honey?" her mother asked in a raised whisper. It shook Lois out of her thoughts and made her look up at her mother guiltily, caught in her act of inquisitive intrusion. Her mother's eyes looked red as though she had been crying and her face was wet. But before she could answer she had been scooped up in to her mother's arms and taken out of the room and back down the steps to where she was supposed to have been supervised by her grandfather. Her mother carried her in to the room, past her sleeping Saba who was snoring negligently in his corner of the room and tucked her into bed without ceremony, except for a kiss on her forehead.

After a short period the singing upstairs stopped and Lois heard a lot of movement on the floorboards above her. The guests seemed to be getting ready to leave, which she thought was unusual for this time of night. She could hear a long line of them walking slowly down the steps at the side of the house in single file and suddenly they were all gone. The only sounds breaking the silence were the comparatively uninteresting and unmelodious sounds of her parents clearing up pots, bowls, cups and jars after the meal.

Lois must have fallen asleep while her parents were still clearing up and at some point, much later that night they were all suddenly woken by anxious shouting in the street outside. It was never really that peaceful in the city, particularly during a festival period when the population swelled to an unsustainable level. There was always someone or something breaking the silence, but the tone of these shouts put them on edge immediately. There was a real panic evident in the voices which triggered an instinctive reaction in case it affected them personally. She could hear people running up the steps to the room above theirs in ones and twos and slamming the door once they were in the room. Her father got out of bed to investigate. He seemed calm because he had expected the guests to return at some later hour, but he went out of the house with a purpose about him just in case there was trouble that had to be dealt with. Lois could hear him talking to the people upstairs. There seemed to be something very wrong and when her father came back into the room he looked worried.

"What is it?" asked her mother who had been sitting up ever since her father had got out of bed. Lois could see the white of her mother's eyes wide with concern in the dork of the room.

"He's been arrested," was all her father said and her mother clasped her hands to her mouth in horror.

"Oh no…" was all her mother could say. She sat there motionless, hands still clasped over her mouth.

"Who has been rested?" Lois asked, not sure what this meant.

"Shush Honey. Go back to sleep," her mother said somewhat predictably. Lois knew there was no point asking again so lay back down in her bed. Though whenever sleep was about to take her there were more hurried footsteps on the cobbles outside then the pattering of sandals running up the steps at the side of the house.

These arrivals continued intermittently over a period of several hours, though the later arrivals did so more stealthily and without any shouting. All the comings and goings unsettled the inhabitants of the house, with the exception perhaps of Saba who snored on untroubled, his poor hearing a blessing on such a night as this.

It was the anxious tone of the conversations they could hear through the floorboards and the panicked running outside that caused the upset. It affected them all.

At one point in the night they could hear the rhythmic stomp of soldiers' hobnailed caligae on the stone paving as they marched by. The room upstairs fell silent for quite a while after that and there was an eerie chill about the night, which made you want to cuddle up to your loved ones for comfort and security and made you pray for daybreak to come.

* * *

It was Saturday morning and Jerusalem had not slept well. The city lay quiet, her head spinning from the excesses she'd hosted and indulged in over the previous twenty four hours. Like a drunk trying to piece together the fragments of her shattered memory, struggling to remember what she'd said and wondering whether she'd gotten away with it. Had her excesses betrayed her? Were her lust-fuelled indulgences going to condemn her in the morning? What would the myriad of her more devout guests that had come for the party think of her now?

Those that had managed to sleep in the city had either slept fitfully or snored noisily, having anesthetised their consciences with wine imbibed for that particular purpose. But they would feel no better for it when morning eventually dragged them from their beds. Outside in her unlit narrow streets, unrest threatened to increase the guilt of the city as insomniacs wandered with aching heads, trying to avoid the more shadowy creatures who preferred the night: the confused troubled drunks, the tougher career prostitutes and their shame-filled or more vicious clients. Those grateful for the dark's facilitation of their sordid activities. There were also the more benign and easily spooked four legged scavengers of the night sniffing in dark recesses of the city for scraps and opportunities.

In the southwest corner of the city squatting on the hillside sat the aspiring splendour of the high priest's home. There Caiaphas lay in his bed, in his chamber on the first floor staring at the dimly lit ceiling, sleep avoiding him as though he were contagion personified. The luxury of his residence and the comfort of his bed would not entice sleep that stubbornly refused to embrace him. Tonight, uncharacteristically, he left the lamp in his room burning to keep some light close by as if to constrain the darkness that had filled his soul and to prevent it from enveloping him utterly. He could not stop his mind from replaying the events of the previous day, over and over. Had they worked out as he had hoped? With the benefit of hindsight, would he have done anything differently? These were events he had consciously been the architect of, cleverly contrived to remove another of his enemies. One who had opposed him to his face and refused to acknowledge his hard earnt authority as his High Priest, which Caiaphas held on to as tightly as his chubby fingers now gripped the blankets about him. Actually, his position was bestowed on him through familial connection, but Caiaphas believed he had earned it. Deserved it. This opponent, this man who had repeatedly humiliated him and what he held dear. Publicly embarrassing him and the best of his scholars and teachers of the law, not by challenging them on points of theology or tradition, but on its application and his endless insistence on involving the wretched and cursed of society in these matters. Why did he insist on bringing the penniless, the diseased, prostitutes and their like into the temple, into his domain? It was beyond charity. It could only have been done with the expressed intent to denigrate what Caiaphas himself and his family had been so careful to construct. He was therefore fully deserving of the most severe punishment, as had been meted out to him yesterday.

But the justice Caiaphas had brought about for himself, brought him no peace and without which the satisfaction that should have been his to enjoy was shallow, insipid and he resented the dead man even more for spoiling this for him too. Even in his death it seemed he taunted him.

Resigning himself to a second night without sleep, Caiaphas attempted some mental gymnastics to skip over the images of the unpleasant gore and horrors of the previous day's executions. He needed to be more positive about the coming day and what this would bring for him. He didn't need to worry himself anymore about the dead son of a carpenter. It takes a particular amalgamation of heart and mind to be able to do this and Caiaphas had given himself the capacity to do it. He had trained himself to vault over obstacles another weaker conscience would stumble over. He could leap over gaps between the principles of theology and the imperatives of the ambitions he harboured. He had climbed the social and political ladders that were within his grasp.

His mind was nimble and far more capable of mastering intellectual challenges than his corpulence would allow him to physically, once it had been hefted off his mattress. But that didn't worry him. Respect was due because of who he was, not for how lithe or strong he was. The robes of his office would ensure that this would continue as surely as he felt they concealed the evidence of his life of indulgence. His weapon of choice was his intellect, which he felt he could wield as effectively as any trained soldier could wield a sword. He could cut his foe down with a single well-chosen word, or with no response at all, his silence speaking volumes about the contempt in which he held his opponent. But that carpenter's son took all his cunning and wit to defeat. There had been moments, and on reflection now Caiaphas reassured himself that these must have been moments of uncharacteristic weakness on his part; when he actually wondered if he would ever win a duel with this man from Nazareth. But he had won through in the end, confident that his reputation remained intact and that was all that mattered now.

* * *

Not far from Caiaphas, in much more humble surroundings, a small group of poor, goodhearted lovers of God lay awake. They, like Caiaphas, lay staring at their ceiling, but broken-hearted and confused. Eyes stinging from the tears that had been shed and for some, tears that still leaked and ran down the sides of the faces, wetting their hair and the rolled garments serving as cushions beneath their heads. Sleep wanted to embrace them but the pain of their loss kept it away and anxiety tugged at them continually, reminding them of the hope that was now lost. Imaginations subject to their growing fears conjured up images of punishments that awaited them next. Eventually, exhausted, some finally succumbed to sleep's embrace in the early hours of this

Saturday morning. Lying in the clothes they had worn all week and on simple mats, without the privacy or the comfort afforded to Caiaphas, they slipped into sleep's waiting arms and were carried away, if only for a short time to the restorative oblivion each so desperately needed.

* * *

The wind that had been gusting all night continued to bother Caiaphas, troubling the shutters at his windows and sighing through the gaps between the wood and the stone walls. It annoyed him, as did so much about his life that wasn't to his liking or under his control. Someone was snoring in the house and this annoyed him too. It sounded like his father-in-law, and why should that old rogue enjoy sleep when it kept its distance from him now? He could hear the guards outside whispering and joking, but not really trying to keep their voices down.

"Disrespectful, lazy imbeciles," he muttered, making a mental note to reprimand the captain of the guard in the morning about their slovenly behaviour. But it was too early for Caiaphas to start the day yet so he lay there, his bad back aching and the blankets that covered him, damp from his sweat, were getting knotted as his tossed back and forth. One minute uncomfortably warm, the next too cold as they exposed him to the chill of the empty night. The blankets annoyed him too and they got slapped and kneaded in angry fistfuls and tugged about him roughly as a consequence.

Outside of the city walls, across the Kidron Valley, Claudia had woken earlier than normal, her sleep interrupted by an uninvited guest who was at this moment sleeping in her makeshift bed. Now that she was awake her hunger drove her to find some breakfast and she busied herself trying to root out something to eat. The guest snored on with no regard for the disruption his presence was causing her. Claudia was young and perfectly formed with beautiful white hair that covered her from the bridge of her nose to the tip of her tail. The young goat's diet, if left to graze freely, would have consisted of the tender tips of shrubs, weeds and plants that grew around the garden where she was now tethered. However, as anyone who has looked after goats will tell you, the animal's natural curiosity will lead it to chew on and taste a variety of materials vaguely resembling vegetation, just to see if they are good to eat. It was this natural curiosity which lead Claudia to taste the bundle rudely snoring in her bed.

Claudia so named by her owners in a rather petty, but self-satisfying act of defiance, after Claudia Procula, the wife of Pontius Pilate. Pilate was the Roman Prefect who had recently moved south to Jerusalem from his base on the coast at Caesarea Maritime. It was partly because of her namesake that Claudia (the goat) was from time to time the unfortunate recipient of some unnecessarily harsh treatment from her frustrated owners, more harsh perhaps than if she had no name at all or something more reverential like Ruth or Esther. The heavy taxation inflicted on the ordinary people of Judea under Roman rule was burdensome and resentment at funding the Roman war machine manifested itself in both open public and private acts of rebellion. The Romans stamped out the more public acts in their own inimitable and well proven fashion. The more private acts of rebellion such as naming your goat after their Prefect's wife were less likely to topple the government, but in the same vein the armies of Rome were less likely to be despatched to snuff it out. This petty flame of resistance consequently burned brightly, at least in this particular household.

Claudia (the goat) would normally spend the night in the house with her owners, however for the past few nights she had been tethered outside because guests from out of town were staying at the house to celebrate the Passover festivities with them. During this night Claudia was once again tethered to a small shelter erected for her to sleep in. However, this morning it was occupied by Simon Peter who was sleeping on the straw her owners had placed there for her bedding the previous week. Claudia's curiosity was no different to other goats' and this morning she was curious about the bundle of material that had appeared during the night and had dislodged her from her bed. It's hard to say what plant his sandal strap reminded her of, or once she had finished chewing it and deciding it was too tough to be edible, what plant his outer robe reminded her off, but both were chewed on and tugged at that morning.

The sampling of the sandal did not appeal to Claudia nor did it rouse Peter, but the tugging at his outer garment did, as the young goat's persistent pulling dislodged it from his sleepy grasp and exposed him to the chilled morning air. The unwelcomed awakening disorientated him momentarily and Peter kicked out with his foot and gruffly muttered something under his breath to discourage whoever it was that was trying to rouse him. The goat, herself having determined that neither sandal nor cloth were desirable supplements to her diet, skipped away with a muted clank of the bell tied around her neck and a bleat of resentment. She moved away from Peter to continue feeding on plants at the furthest extent of her immediate tethering.

Peter had spent his second night in the open air, alone and away from the group of his closest friends, which is how he came to be sleeping in this crude and smelly shelter constructed on the edge of a small olive grove to the east of Jerusalem. This Saturday morning was hateful and dawned sullenly. Devoid of colour, the sky wept a cold, grey light which did nothing to dispel the blackness which had not left Peter for the past two days, nor the sour hollow feeling in the pit of his stomach. He felt compelled to stay out on his own, unwilling to return to the company of his friends because of the crushing weight of shame and guilt that his actions once again brought down upon him. He couldn't bear the thought of the conversation he imagined going on in the upstairs room of the house where the group had been staying. The crying, the pacing up and down, the misery, the handwringing… and he had done nothing to prevent it happening. It was this overwhelming sense of impotence, the feelings of helplessness and hopelessness that had kept him away from the group. The thought of the vain, hollow, baseless hope he knew some would offer in the face of their loss angered him. Truths were regurgitated without understanding in the hope they would somehow gel into a reality that would save them from the pain of this hour. "Truths" received with joy in the light of life when it felt like nothing could stand in the way of the coming kingdom of God now lacked meaning in the cold, grey morning of their loss. On the day when the truth was meant to carry them, comfort and console them. Truths like the heady aroma of home cooking heralding a feast that is about to be enjoyed by everyone, instead now seemed to be food for others to enjoy, not for them, even though they starved for its comfort in their time of pain. All this just jarred with him like someone singing loudly off key. He then started to get angry as he ran and re-ran the imaginary conversations over and over again in his mind. So much so that he had to stay away from the group lest he said or did something else that he would also later regret. Regret… he had his share of that right now. Why are the lives of some so peppered with regrets, yet others appear to sail serenely through life seemingly untroubled, never regretting a decision or missing an opportunity?

"Why were some happy to delude themselves with a baseless hope?" "If it wasn't grounded in any fundamental core of faith, or knowledge, it was just a fundamental inability to face facts." The reality Peter was looking at now was that all was lost, because Messiah had been crucified and everyone knew a crucified Messiah was a failed Messiah.

Peter had spent all of Friday outside of the city, but judiciously avoided the north and west of the city, spending most of his time to the east, wandering between Jerusalem, Bethany and Bethpage, lost in his dark thoughts and self-recriminations. However, as he walked along the top of the Mount of Olives these places started to overlook the murderous scenes to the north of the city, so he had to turn back towards the south, all the time keeping his head covered and looking at his feet to avoid eye contact with anyone who might recognise him and want to engage him in conversation. He could no longer be that celebrated someone he evidently wasn't going to be anymore, or answer questions he just didn't want to face. He knew back at home that people had thought him an unlikely disciple of a Rabbi. When he and Andrew had given up their fishing business to follow Jesus there were plenty who muttered behind their backs that this was a foolish and irresponsible action for Peter to take. He was a married man and had a family to provide for. He was a good fisherman, ran a good business around Galilee, but was no more suited to being a disciple of a Rabbi than he was likely of becoming a mother of twins. They knew him as being unschooled in religious affairs and occasionally reckless. This desire of his to follow Jesus of Nazareth was bound to end in disaster... and oh how right they were. If they could see him now: Jesus dead and he wandering about on his own trying to avoid people, sleeping in a goat's bed. Separated from his friends, more dishevelled than usual, smelling strongly of goat and not knowing what to do next. Oh how they would shake their heads at one another and say, "What a shame"!! "What a shame for the family, for the wife. Such a good girl. She did not deserve such a foolish husband. We said God had never fashioned him for such a life. He was a strong boy yes, but intellectually, academically...? No, no, no... not a clever boy. Nice, yes. Kind boy, but not clever."

Although he had not stuck around to witness it after the arrest on Thursday night, there was no mistaking the fate of Jesus. This man who had so completely changed Peter's life. The man who the authorities had hounded, schemed against, and had finally snatched late that night. Already condemned to a shameful death before they had condescended to act out the farce of a trial to legitimise their verdict.

There had been an unpleasant buzz in and around the city that Friday. It was like the angry buzz of flies fussing over a dead carcass, contrasted with the healthy buzz the city normally had at Passover, especially when Jesus was there bringing the essential life force of God into the city's festivities. His love and grace, His strength in the face of the pompous religious 'elite'. At these times the city had a healthy buzz. In his mind he contrasted the imagery of the flies feeding on filth with the productive buzz of bees making honey. The former a foul, self-indulgent swarm, a consequence of death, the latter healthy and productive, bringing forth such sweetness. Jerusalem had changed for him now…

When he first met Jesus, Peter had been too afraid to stand in His presence, becoming too aware of his own sinfulness, certain Jesus could see all he had done and would condemn him for it. It was not that Jesus had ever condemned Him, rather it was just a product of standing in the presence of someone so good, so loving, and so holy that he felt unworthy to even breathe the same air as Him. His own shortcomings were never so apparent in the company of friends and family who were not so different to himself. This Jesus was different though, as different as day is from night. But the more he spent time with Him, the more he felt his unconditional love and acceptance and rather than wanting to flee, he wanted to follow and draw nearer to Him. Jesus also had this belief in him, which was as unexpected as it was unfamiliar to Simon Bar Jonah, the clumsy uneducated fisherman. Jesus had a certainty that notwithstanding his failings he could… no… he *would* be the perfect disciple to help him bring the Kingdom of Heaven to Earth. Surely Jesus was mistaken. He couldn't think of anything else he was wrong about, but he had clearly got this wrong... The contrast was clear this Saturday morning… Jesus had been wrong about this one thing: him.

Peter could not now imagine a life without Him though, but this was the life he was now staring at this morning.

The day before, as people scurried past him on the road there was a perverse air of exhilaration, an excitable fear. Agitated. Definitely confused. Some gossiped, some cried; the young and the stupid revelled in the scandal of the day's events. Some were eager to share the latest and most scandalous news they'd heard for a very long time with any that would make the mistake of greeting them and giving them the opportunity to pass on and revel in the bad news they carried. The great prophet from Galilee had finally been caught by the authorities and was being put to death. Have you ever heard of such a thing…? Well, yes sadly; it was all too common under this oppressive regime, but that answer was seldom given, so the bad news thrived and grew.

Even with his head covered and face down these people wanted Peter's attention so they could share what they knew. "Had he heard the news of what was happening in the city today?" Peter didn't respond. He never fed their desire to revel in their sensuous gossip about this latest foul act of Pilate. For a time Peter had considered starting out for home by himself, but greater than his desire to leave the city was his sense of duty to his fellow travellers; those he had travelled south with from Galilee the week before. Those who depended on his help for their journey back, which now threatened to be so much more perilous since Jesus had been condemned as an enemy of the state, than it had been on their route down to Jerusalem for the festival. It was partly this innate characteristic of Peter's, his sense of obligation to support and protect others that prevented him from leaving. That and the inevitability that even if he did head off by himself they would eventually catch up with him back in his home in Capernaum. These friends and neighbours of his would remain his life-long friends and neighbours until death parted them.

They were inextricably bound together through family and community ties. Many of them had grown up with each other, worked together, fished on the lake together and eaten together. They had been to each other's family weddings, celebrated the births of each other's children and mourned together as they buried their dead. They had laughed and cried together and more recently, since meeting, Jesus had travelled the length and breadth of the country with him together, travelling to places they would never otherwise have visited. But they had also met people and lived with those which, if given the choice, he would probably not normally have acknowledged if he'd walked past them on the road.

It was the life they shared: their history together as a group and as individuals since meeting Jesus that bound the disciples together. Their shared experiences, the wonders they had witnessed being done in the Name of God and the teachings that made their hearts burn and their heads spin as they tried to digest it. All this drew them together as one body formed from diverse backgrounds into one common calling. For now though, the voice that had done the calling had been silenced.

So it was that these ties, this calling and his early morning hunger which was now gnawing away at him, drawing him back to the upper room above the tavern where the rest of the group were probably spending the Sabbath. Peter had not eaten since Thursday night and this compounded his emotional state. Not that he could be so analytical about this, but he did need to eat, so he decided to head back to join what was left of the group. Back to face his friends and their inevitable questions, which whilst born out of a love for him, right now felt like an undeserved, unwarranted concern given his desertion and denial of Jesus on Thursday night. The questions he imagined were therefore too much for him. It would feel like they would be prying even if they weren't. He was afraid that in answering the caring, mostly innocuous questions they would ultimately uncover the true Peter. The weak Peter. The Peter he hoped he would never allow to be seen again. The Peter he hated. The frightened one who had scuttled away from his friend on the night of the arrest. Abandoning him to save his own skin. He could hear their questions now…

"Where have you been?"

"What happened to you? Are you okay?"

"We thought you had been arrested too."

"Have you been arrested…?"

"What did they do to you?" … and so on…

Peter yawned, stretched his aching muscles and shuddered as he sat on the low wall and swung his legs over to stand in the road on the other side. He left the olive grove where he had spent the long night unable to sleep, except for a couple of hours snatched early in the morning. To start with he had sat with his back to the gnarled trunk of what must have been the most uncomfortable olive tree in all of Israel. It was the same tree he, James and John had sat under the night Jesus had been arrested. Sleep did not seem to have eluded them that night, as they'd struggled to stay awake, but it would not come on Friday night when in some childish hope Peter fantasized that if he just closed his eyes in the same spot, by some miracle time would be reversed and he would be allowed to re-live that awful Thursday night differently, but it could never be thus. Later, desperately in need of sleep, he had wrapped his robe around himself, booted Claudia out of her shelter and lay down on the straw with his back to the low wall to keep out of the cold wind and eventually got some rest. Just the way a drunk seeks oblivion from cheap wine.

Now as he headed down the road that led him back across the Kidron valley towards the city, the cold wind that had bothered him all night had dropped to a gentler breeze, but there was no warmth in it to ease his aching bones, or to drive the night's damp out of his clothes. Nothing in it to comfort him, to ease his aching heart or clear his dull, aching head. He tried to run his thick fingers through his black unkempt hair, trying to look a little less dishevelled than he knew he did. The knots in his hair made him wince as he forced his fingers through them. Breaking their tangles, he then repeated the action to try and make the unknotted recalcitrant fibres lie flat against his scalp.

As he worked his way down the empty road the temple loomed large before him: the fantastic central structure of the Holy of Holies towering above the city walls in all its dreadful, awe inspiring splendour. An architectural wonder that rivalled anything of its time. The temple was the scene of so many confrontations between Jesus and the religious leaders: the teachers of the law, the chief priests, Pharisees, Sadducees and all their many and varied zealous hangers on. Jesus, Peter reflected, never seemed to be in awe of the stonework or the lavish use of precious metal and gems used in the building of this wonder; only with the God it was intended to honour. His Father.

As he walked along the road with the immense structure on his right, dwarfing him, Peter could imagine the priests now, no doubt congratulating themselves on a job well done yesterday, getting rid of their most outspoken and embarrassing opponent. It had been a hurriedly coordinated and unlikely alliance formed of their own disparate parties and the Romans, but an alliance which seemed to have borne fruit. Who would have thought that likely?

The conviction was successfully secured, albeit at night with questionable legality, but no one was going to mention that now. The end justified the means, and the end in this case was the end of the problem called 'Jesus of Nazareth'. That was all that mattered. This could only bode well for a better and more peaceful life for the religious community as a whole. Maybe they had shown themselves to be trustworthy in the eyes of the Romans in this joint venture? Maybe this would buy them more autonomy, more freedom, perhaps even a more secure future for their temple, their livelihood. This would suit them for the time being at least. Once God answers their nation's prayers and sends their deliverer Messiah, he will set them free from this yoke of oppression, he will lead a victorious army and drive out these filthy, gentile pigs and restore the former glory of Israel. But for now though they would feel that at least they had gained some level of respect from them by this rare act of cooperation in achieving the common goal: getting rid of this jumped up carpenter and would-be prophet from Nazareth.

The simple truth eluded them that the outcome from their actions from the previous few days had resulted in the death of their very hoped-for-Messiah and it was *His* blood, not their *oppressors'*, that now lay congealed in dark pools at the site of his execution. The nails they had asked to be driven through the flesh of their infuriating opponent, to shut him up once and for all, were driven through the hands and feet of the Saviour they longed for. This fact that was hidden from them and would not distract them from their continued dreaming of their day of salvation, nor would it dampen their now vain hope.

Peter's perception of what was going on inside the temple courts behind those walls was as wrong as his progress along the road was slow. Maybe the thoughts and attitudes existed, but the various religious factions had gathered within the inner courts, outside the holy of holies and were in furious debate. Their focus being on the meaning of the torn curtain, or, for some, whether it had any meaning at all. Wasn't it just a consequence of yesterday's minor earthquake? "We've had bigger earthquakes before but this has never happened before…" one old priest protested. "…and the sun turning dark at the same hour, shall we ignore that too?" said another. The fact that the sun's light was eclipsed at the same time as the earthquake and the curtain tearing was an awkward coincidence that was difficult to ignore or to explain away; but Jesus' most hard-nosed, expert opponents did their best to do just that. There could not be anything but a unanimous acceptance that the outcome from their actions, the death of the Jesus of Nazareth, was anything but a triumph. The minor damage sustained could not, would not detract from this.

There then followed characteristically fierce opposing views about how or whether the curtain should be repaired, who should be commissioned to repair it, what ceremonial preparation would be required of those who would be involved in its repair, and so on. On and on the arguments would go in a way that only religious institutions can cultivate them. Supremely missing their raison d'etre, their mission to the people, their purpose for being with their focus turned wholly on themselves. The longer the arguments went on, the wider the divisions became and deeper the trenches were dug, from which opposing beliefs became encamped, defended and justified.

This temple built to the glory of the one true, good and Holy God once again became the scene of yet another graceless, unholy dispute. In this respect, this morning was no different to so many others that had preceded it. In every other respect, this morning was like no other since the beginning of time. They had killed the One who they were waiting for. Their hoped for Messiah now lay very cold and very dead in a tomb outside the city. Tried and convicted by an illegitimate council, convened under cover of night. His sentence determined by his judges before any case could be established against him. The focus of repairing the torn curtain was a welcome distraction for those involved in the prosecution of Jesus as well as for those who stood silently by and allowed the injustice to happen. Thoughts of whether there was any symbolism in the torn curtain were put aside and would not be perpetuated after its repair and definitely not discussed openly once the matter had been dealt with.

The fact that Jesus had often claimed the only way to God was *through* Him was another inconvenient coincidence right now. The curtain, which kept all but the chief priest from entering into the presence of God, was torn from top to bottom, as if to open the way for anyone who wanted to do so, to come into the presence of God. For this reason alone the curtain had to be repaired and immediately. To restore order, restore tradition and to restore their control of who could and could not enter into the presence of their God. *Their* God? It seemed that their God no longer wished to be encountered by the few and had left the holy of holies, tearing the curtain in the process. But the work started that morning to metaphorically repair the 'stable door' after the Divine had bolted. In some places of worship, that work continues still at the hands of a few who want to maintain an impression that the way to God can only be found through the hands of a privileged few.

Peter's progress back to the house of Ahaz was deliberately slow, giving himself time to formulate responses to the questions he was anticipating. It wasn't so much that these questions were necessarily unwelcome; it was the attention he would get. He did not want to be the centre of attention, he did not deserve to be. Neither did he want to face his own unanswered questions that had been tormenting him since Thursday night.

"How could he have denied Jesus the way he did?"

"Why was he suddenly terrified of being associated with Jesus?"

"Why did that young servant girl's questions scare him so? She was just a kid…"

"How could all of Jesus' disciples have deserted him in his hour of need?"

As grey as the morning was, it was easier to bear than the darkness which had brought the accusing thoughts all night. Daylight brought a perspective that night denied him. The feelings of shame and self-disgust remained, but as the dull light of day had started to dawn, the torment started to ease, ever so slightly.

Peter's thoughts were momentarily interrupted by a sharp and surprisingly cheerful "Good morning! God's blessings be upon you brother!" Peter looked up and saw the bright, expectant, mostly toothless face of one of the city's many beggars, sitting by the roadside on a crude mat of old palm branches. "You are about your business early this morning, Sir," Mephibosheth continued, cheerfully. "Could you spare some bread or a few coins for a poor hungry beggar, Sir?"

As if being startled from a deep sleep, Peter was momentarily disorientated. "Sorry, I have no food, my friend. Neither do I have any money," and to illustrate this Peter drew back his cloak and patted the flaccid empty pouch on his belt, showing the man where he would have kept his money if he'd had any. However, as he patted it there was the faintest of incriminating clinks, which wasn't missed by the bat-like hearing of the beggar attracting his beady gaze, like a hawk locked on to a juicy mouse which had unwisely broken cover. The unmistakeable clink, albeit almost inaudible gave the lie to the statement Peter had just unintentionally made.

"Ooh… hang on…" Peter said, untying the pouch. "I might have something…" He probed the depths of the pouch with his index finger and thumb and withdrew all that was in there: three small misshapen bronze prutah. Coins of little worth to him but would feed Mephibosheth for another day. Peter bent down and dropped them into the man's small pot, but no sooner were the coins dropped into the pot than they were hurriedly scooped out with his crooked fingers and hidden in a cloth beneath his tangled limbs. As he was doing so the beggar pronounced another toothless blessing over Peter, before his attention was drawn to another unsuspecting traveller trudging up the hill towards the city. The encounter with the beggar was refreshingly normal for Peter: low key and largely unchallenging and as small as the good deed was, it helped revive him a little.

Peter turned to continue on his way up the slope and just as he was leaving he felt compelled to make the moment last a little longer by giving Mephibosheth some trite encouragement before he left: "There… you are now officially wealthier than I am!" But as he walked on he could hear the beggar had not heard him as he was already addressing his next customer with the same patter he'd used on Peter and probably everyone else who would walk within earshot that morning: "Good morning Brother! God's blessings be upon you…you are about your business early this morning." Peter then winced as he heard the sharp words being exchanged between the two men as rather than being the recipient to the beggar's blessing it sounded like the traveller's household were being singled out for some rather unpleasant disasters to befall them because the 'customer' had not responded in the manner hoped for by the beggar and curses rather than blessings were his reward.

As Peter walked on he spotted a group of four soldiers on the road ahead, it was an immediate reminder of the threat that he may now face as a follower of the man they had just executed. Fortunately, three of the four men were leaning on their spears, listening to the fourth telling them some unwholesome story, gesticulating wildly as he acted out his tale. He had them so entranced they paid no attention to Peter. Not wishing to encounter any more soldiers than was absolutely necessary, Peter immediately changed his pace and resolved to take a more direct route back to the upper room. Sticking mainly to the damp, shadowy alleyways that threaded their way through the old city, like veins on a leaf, Peter wound his way in the approximate direction of the house. Although not a native of the city he knew the general direction he needed to take, which would bring him out on to the more familiar main routes, thus reducing his risk of encountering anyone who could make trouble for him. The most direct route from Gethsemane back in to the city to the house of Ahaz would be via a long flight of stone steps that ran adjacent to the house of Caiaphas. Peter understandably opted for a more circuitous route rather than choosing to venture anywhere near there again.

He eventually arrived without incident at the foot of the steps that led to the upper room of the house owned by Ahaz, the man Peter only really knew as the large generous inn keeper Jesus had befriended. And Peter was thankful for that.

HIDING IN THE UPPER ROOM

The steps to the upper room ran up the outside of the end wall of the two storey town house that Ahaz used the ground floor of as a tavern. There was nothing particularly unusual about the building in its time. It was characteristic of many of those in the city, but less common in Galilee where single storey, single roomed dwellings were the norm, particularly among the lower classes.

Peter climbed the steps to the upper room unsteadily and tried the door at the top. It was closed and could not be opened. The seeds of paranoia that had been sown when he saw the soldiers outside the city had germinated and were starting to thrive as he stood conspicuously (he felt) at the top of the steps. He thought that he might be being watched by some unseen enemy and becoming fearful of this imagined threat he faced by remaining outside, Peter tried opening the door once more. He drew a deep breath, lifted the catch and leant harder against the door. This attempt elicited some movement on the other side of the door with some loud whispers for people to be quiet. There was a hushed pause until he heard the familiar voice of John.

"Who is it? What do you want?"

"It's me, Simon," Peter said. Peter used his natural given name rather than the one Jesus had bestowed on him. The name Peter seemed to herald promise, whereas his given name Simon was used when things were not going so well for him, when he allowed stupidity or impetuosity to get the better of him.

"Peter?" John asked

"Yes."

"Could you let me in please?"

"Of course, of course! Oh thank God you're alright."

There then came the sound of scraping from behind the door as if heavy items were being dragged away and hissed questions from deeper within the room enquiring about the identity of the person outside. Clearly the seeds of paranoia had found fertile soil in a number of the group, not just Peter.

The ill-fitting door flexed then shuddered open on its crude hinges. Peter was greeted by a very relieved John peering round the door at him, and if only for a fraction of a second, Peter noticed John look beyond him into the street below as if checking for something. John pulled the door wide and opened his arms to embrace his beloved friend. The two hugged, holding each other for much longer than they would normally, John letting the embrace crush the anxiety out of himself that he had been feeling about the fate of his dear friend and Peter trying to crush the shame that he had felt so acutely, now starting to dissipate because he was back in the arms of his good friend. However, the stain Peter carried was more resilient and required a moment alone with his Lord at a later date to be cleansed completely. For now though it was good to be back in the bosom of his family.

The women in the room made a fuss of Peter and immediately set about making sure he was fed. They invited him to sit nearer to the brazier, which had been brought inside, so that he could warm himself.

As he gratefully ate the bread, dried figs and some dates given to him, he answered the various questions he had anticipated with his readily prepared and well-rehearsed answers.

"Yes, I am fine, just a bit tired and hungry."

"No, I was not arrested."

"I had not been staying anywhere, I just needed to be alone…" he was going to add "with God" but that would have been fake piety which he hated, so he stopped before saying anything he didn't mean.

"I needed to…." he started, then stopped. "The previous few months and years have been…" he tried, then stopped again. Then after a pause he said, "I am truly sorry for giving you cause for concern. It was selfish of me." His gaze dropped and he stared at the food in his hands.

As Peter's eyes adjusted to the low light in the room he looked around at the concerned faces watching him satisfy his hunger. Now he was eating he realised just how hungry he had become. Some of the twelve were there. Judas was missing, as were James and Thomas… John could see Peter making a mental inventory of all who were and were not there said he had not seen or heard of Judas since Thursday night. James had just gone out into the city to try and get information on the whereabouts of Thomas, and of course Peter. Many of the group of disciples were still unaccounted for since Thursday night. Some of the wider circle of disciples were there with them, as were all the women who had travelled down from Galilee. And there at the back of the room was the heartrending presence of Mary, Jesus' mother surrounded by a handful of women comforting and quietly grieving with her.

"How do you comfort a mother who has witnessed what she has just witnessed?" Peter wondered, though there were many mothers, sisters and widows in Israel who had seen sons, husbands, brothers, fathers tortured to death by the Romans in this way.

The group was much reduced in number, compared to that which had travelled down to Jerusalem and shared the final meal together on the Thursday night, when Peter was last with them. He could make no judgement on this as he himself had been missing for some time and had contemplated returning to Galilee by himself. He suspected some had kept running, following the scuffle in the olive grove the night Jesus had been arrested in Gethsemane. They may well be on their way home already. This flock, as Jesus liked to refer to them, really had been scattered when he was arrested.

John said some were either out in the neighbourhood somewhere or trying to get the latest news on the streets to assess what kind of risks the group now faced, following the unlikely alliance between the Romans and the priests to effect the arrest of Jesus. John admitted that some were out trying to determine Peter's fate, thinking he had probably been arrested as well. This stung Peter and just added in his own mind to the weight of the prosecution case against him. How could he have been so thoughtless? Others were now in danger because of him. John could see this and said he knew where they had gone, so he turned to a couple of young men who were sat closest to him and asked them if they would go and call the men back, now that Peter was safely back with them.

Notwithstanding the joy at seeing Peter's safe return, there was understandably not the usual happy banter that accompanied this crowd of believers now. There was no retelling of what they had been witnesses to, which was their usual fare after having spent a day working with Jesus. No retelling of old stories. There was just this hollow, empty sense of loss that sat in the pit of all their stomachs and ate the joy that had given them life. It tethered their hearts once free like sparrows, enjoying crumbs that fell from their Master's table, flitting and playing with one another, but now no longer able to enjoy that "normality". No longer able to think about whatever it was they used to think about, because of yesterday. They couldn't look at each other in the eye for any period of time without returning their gaze to the floor and taking a profound interest in pushing meaningless bits of grit about with their feet, or pulling at a loose thread from their tunic, each lost in their own thoughts. Each wishing they had done more and each running through various "if only" scenarios in their minds. All desperately yearned for the comfort of Jesus with them once more. Everything was different without him. Everything reminded them of him. Some were questioning their own actions from the previous couple of days, surprised at how quickly they had fled after the arrest. Not one was proud of their actions. The confidence they had in their own and each other's commitment to the cause had dissipated like the morning mist. All were wondering what the future now held for them.

Silence and gloom sat in their midst as if they were the two newest recruits to the group, relishing the opportunity of joining the band of believers which these two new members had previously been excluded from. They now audaciously aspired to take the place of Jesus as the focal point and for the time being were successful at their task.

Of all of the believers, John seemed to possess something that kept him more animated than the others. It was as if he had some secret insight, some hope that the others were not privy to. Similarly Jesus' mother possessed something the other women did not. Notwithstanding the pain she must have been going through, she exuded an inner peace, a strength that was not evident in those around her. It was as if she accepted this moment. As if she *expected* this moment. In spite of the ache in her heart there was some characteristic unwavering air of holy devotion and submission about her. Her demeanour was having an effect on those around her, especially on the younger women who looked up to her reverentially. The grief was real and heartfelt, but hadn't deteriorated into the wailing and wallowing in misery that was customary in some parts. She was gentle of spirit, as her son had been. Her heart sought her God's as her son's had in every circumstance, and as trying as this day was, it was evident that she sought her Lord in this moment too.

Peter felt better for the food he'd been given and when he had finished eating, John motioned to him that he wanted to speak with him privately. Privacy wasn't going to be easy in this busy room and neither felt they could wander the city in safety yet, so John asked a couple of the younger men if they wouldn't mind giving up their corner so he and Peter could have some space. They gladly cleared their things so Peter and John could sit down and they moved to the other side of the room. Joanna handed the two men a cup of water each as they sat down, then she too moved away to let the two of them talk, respecting the privacy the two men needed.

John was the first to speak. He wanted to make sure Peter knew exactly what had happened to Jesus, conscious as he was that Peter had been absent from most of it. John had stayed as close as he dared throughout the events of Thursday night and Friday. From time to time as he described the events John lost his composure and his voice broke and tears filled his eyes. As he described the farce of the trial he couldn't contain his anger at the hypocrisy of the religious hierarchy who he saw as having choreographed the whole event. How they danced around their rituals and customs so they could preserve their appearance of "cleanliness", while utterly compromising themselves on the fundamentals of the Law and judicial process to secure the death of an innocent man who'd become an embarrassment to them.

The brutality the Romans subjected Jesus to caused both men to cry as John tried to retell it. Peter had heard the blows thudding into Jesus from where he stood below in the courtyard of Caiaphas' house. Crunching blows and slaps sounded like butchers preparing meat in the market place as they broke up an animal's carcass for sale. The violence was distressing, but the cold absence of compassion from those who delivered it was chilling. No personal injustice motivating them, but a cold dark hatred for their victim fuelling a determined persistence that would not stop until instructed to.

The brutality of the Romans was nothing new to Peter or John. Crucified bodies were hard to avoid since their occupation of the land. Oh how they loved to nail up constant visual reminders of the fate that awaited anyone who would dare to oppose them. Many of the main thoroughfares around the country had been turned into macabre, corpse lined boulevards.

Peter had seen where things were headed while he was still in the courtyard. He'd heard the heavy blows hitting Jesus as they questioned him. Each painful dull thud and slap accompanied by hate-filled accusation spat in Jesus' face. Each blow struck his own heart, slapped his own face. He could feel their spittle as if it was trickling down his own face. He imagined their hot, foul breath, wreaking of sour wine in his own nostrils and couldn't bear to witness it anymore. John's account brought back the trauma of it all too acutely.

"The last I saw of you, you were below me in the courtyard." John said. "What happened to you? I was worried that they'd decided to arrest you for striking that odious wretch Malchus in the olive grove.

"No. Although some did recognise me from that scuffle, maybe the fact that the Lord healed him right then and there saved me from any further repercussions. I am so sorry I did that. It could have become so much worse for all of us and I am so sorry that I ran off.

"You don't owe me any apology Peter, but tell me, why did you leave? Was it getting too dangerous for you down there in the courtyard? I think being acquainted with the family of Caiaphas afforded me some immunity, but I don't know how much longer I am going to benefit from that.

"You would think I ran because I got some rough treatment from some of the guards, wouldn't you?" Peter was staring at the floor now. "No. The big man that I am was scared by a poor little serving girl, who meant me no harm. She, like some of the others, thought she recognised me and…" Peter paused "…and I told them all they were wrong. I denied knowing Jesus. I said I didn't know what they were talking about… I actually said I didn't know the man" Peter's voice broke as he confessed this to John. John sat in silence and put his arm around the big man as he started to sob. "I said it three times John! Just to make it absolutely clear that I did not know him." he spluttered through his tears. "Three times John! Three times…" John just held him.

Others in the room paid them little attention. Many of them had shed tears over the past twenty four hours and none had played a role in the recent events that any were particularly proud of.

After a time, John spoke: "I remember hearing Jesus telling you that you would do that. I didn't say anything at the time. There was nothing for me to say. It was none of my business. He always knew us full well. He was never wrong. None of us saw this happening to him. Not with the savage intensity that it did. He said it would happen this way, but we could not countenance it happening. Not to him. Not to one so undeserving of it."

John changed the tack of the conversation slightly away from Peter's immediate pain. "It was as if all the devils of hell were let loose yesterday and the Lord was the focus of their hatred," John reflected. "The Romans and the religious leaders were their willing vassals eager to carry out their foul bidding."

"The whole city was afflicted," Peter finally observed, trying to regain his composure. "There was all manner of dark things going on around the city. Wherever I went I could hear people crying out as if they had been robbed, others crying that they had been assaulted. I heard women screaming from somewhere, I don't know where… It's like the gates of hell opened and dumped its filth in this city. There was just an overspill of darkness all around… and I feel it still."

"I know what you mean," said John. "I felt it too."

Just then James and two other disciples were let through the door.

"Peter!" James exclaimed, as he strode over to where the two men sat. He crouched down so he could embrace his friend before he could stand. "We have been so worried about you. Are you alright? You're looking a bit the worse for wear, my friend."

"Thank you. I'm okay. It's good to see you too."

"Where did you go, James?" John asked, changing the focus of the conversation away from Peter now that they were no longer alone and to save his friend repeating everything he'd just told him.

"I thought I'd go up to the temple courts to see what was happening there."

"Really?" John and Peter were both surprised at James's disregard for his own safety.

"... and..?"

"There was quite a commotion. Which made it easier for me to move about without being noticed. The attention of all the great and the good there was focussed on the damage to the curtain before the Holy of Holies. Do you know it is ripped from top to bottom?"

"Ripped? How? Who did that?" asked John.

"They were saying it happened yesterday afternoon. About three o'clock," James said

No one said anything, but John was immediately struck by the significance if the timing of the tear, occurring as it seems it did around the same time as Jesus was gulping his last painful breath as he died on the cross.

"Was there any other damage done to the temple?"

"Not from what I could make out."

Their reflections were interrupted by another urgent knocking on the door. It was a breathless Martha and her sister Mary. Both looked flushed as they were carrying bundles of what looked like food and had probably been walking as quickly as was decent all the way from Bethany, trying not to draw attention to themselves on the Sabbath.

"Mary, Martha! What are you doing here?" exclaimed one of the women sitting near the brazier. "It's the Sabbath. You could get into all sorts of trouble carrying these loads in broad daylight!"

"Well, we thought you'd need it. Anyway we tried to make the bundles look like babies," she smiled nervously. "There's a lot of you here and I don't know what money you have left," Martha offered. "Has anyone seen Judas?" she continued making the obvious connection between his disappearance and their lack of money with which to buy provisions.

"No," was the unhappy response from those who sat near the door.

"Well, this should see you through for now. We'll bring more tomorrow when it will be easier to do so."

"Thank you and God bless you both for your kindness. You too Lazarus." They shifted their attention from the two women to their brother Lazarus who had just entered the room, carrying a bag of flour that looked every bit like a bag of flour dangling from his right hand. He had made no effort to try and disguise his load, much to the annoyance of his sisters, but in his defence he said he'd rather face the consequences of carrying this on the Sabbath than pretending to look like a mother with a child. He dropped the bag by the wall near the brazier ready to be converted into food that evening once the Sabbath was over. He blinked as his eyes adjusted to the low lit room and greeted those he recognised.

Peter, James and John remained in that corner of the room and discussed the events of the previous day and what they should do to ensure the safety of the group.

One thing Peter was not aware of was what had happened to Jesus' body. He was concerned the Romans had left it hanging on the cross in full public display as was their normal practice and was keen to bring it down.

John told him, "Joseph and Nicodemus, with a couple of others, took him down just before the Sabbath started. Thankfully, on this occasion we have benefitted from the religious hypocrisy that abounds. They didn't want the bodies left on the crosses, so they could celebrate their Passover untroubled. I think it suited them to hide the evidence of their crime as quickly as they could."

"Unbelievable!" said Peter, disgusted at the extent to which the Chief Priests and Pharisees managed to manipulate scripture and tradition to suit their own ends, every time. Then for clarity he asked, "Which Joseph?"

"… of Arimathea."

"Really ..?" Peter was surprised. He knew Jesus had followers among the rich and poor alike and also among some members of the Sanhedrin, but most of these, like Nicodemus, did not like to publicly acknowledge their belief that Jesus was the Son of God for fear of recriminations from the other members.

"What have they done with him?" Peter asked.

"You know Joseph has that garden on the north side of the city?" John asked Peter.

"Yes, I think so. He's got a vineyard there, right?"

"Yes," said John "Right next to Golgotha."

Peter remembered walking through it on a previous visit to the city and nodded to indicate his recognition of where John was describing.

"No more than a stone's throw from where they killed him," said John. "Anyway, they have put him in the tomb that Joseph has there. It's new, it's clean and as far as tombs go it's quite grand, I suppose. Far better than anything we could have afforded to do for him. The tomb is on private land, so it's about as secure as it can be."

"Good…" Peter closed his eyes and buried his head in his hands and sighed deeply. His head swam with graphic images of violence and dead bodies. "What had become of them? Why did it have to come to this? Wasn't there a path they could have taken which would not have led to this... this monstrous end? Didn't God care? How could this be His will?" And so the unanswerable questions swirled around his tired mind with emotions and images he did not want to see anymore.

After a time John looked at Peter and said, "James was right. You are not looking too good my friend. Why don't you lie down and get some rest. You look like you haven't slept for a week."

The food, the warmth of the room and dim light had all started to have its effect on Peter. He thanked his friend for his love and concern and accepted his offer to get some rest. He actually needed some oblivion in the hope that when he woke his mind would have put order to all the confusion that slopped about inside his head and that the sick pain that clung to his heart would somehow have been washed away. He moved the cushion he'd been sitting on into the corner of the room and used it as a pillow. He turned his face to the wall, pulled his knees up to his chest and waited for sleep to take him away. But as tired as he was, sleep was again slow in coming. The images continued to swirl behind his eyelids. Bloodied bodies, discoloured corpses and the shrouded body of his friend, leaking its life blood through the cloth he was wrapped in. The laughter and ridicule of the victors, the sounds of the beatings he'd heard in the courtyard echoing again and again through his mind. His imaginings were not far from the facts.

He screwed his eyes shut more tightly and pressed his thumb and forefingers into his eyes, trying to erase the images with the stars and coloured spots that came from putting pressure on them. Closing his eyes seemed to increase the volume of the noise of conversations going on around the room, which up to that point had only existed as a background murmur. Snippets of each conversation reached him, each overlaying the other. Some were repeating things Jesus had told them a long time ago. Everything he had said seemed to have taken place a long time ago now. A life-time ago. He had said something about how he was going to be killed by sinful men and how if we wanted to follow him we would have to choose to suffer the same. Something about taking up our own crosses and following him. That brought back painful memories for Peter and as sleep started to settle on him and as his mind eventually started to quieten, he recalled this particular event they were talking about. It was another inglorious moment for Peter and the memory of it brought another stab of regret to a heart that was being repeatedly stabbed over and over again.

On that particular day they had been walking with Jesus through some towns and villages in the hills to the north of Galilee. The trips between the various villages they visited were not too arduous as they were all fairly close together. The day had been bright, but the sun not too punishing. As they were on the outskirts of one of these villages they had stopped under the shade of some leafy fig trees and the sunlight just dappled the ground about them. Cicadas rasped lazily in the trees above them. Just when they had settled to enjoy the moment's rest, Jesus asked them who people thought he was. It was an unusual question to ask and it caught them all off guard. Jesus seemed to have a knack for doing this. As usual, they tried to figure out *why* Jesus was asking them this question, so they could give him the answer they thought he was looking for. The trouble with being caught off guard like this was that you invariably did not have time to formulate an acceptable response. The group started by sharing some of the identities they'd heard other people give to Jesus. Peter remembered his suspicions that some of their company were just sharing their own misunderstandings, pretending they'd heard someone else saying it, thereby avoiding embarrassment in front of their companions if they were way off the mark; as they all so often found themselves.

They were all in awe of Jesus. No one had seen anyone do the things he had done, or heard teaching like his, so some assorted, half-baked ideas were shared, because where the miraculous had become an everyday thing in his company, anything seemed plausible.

"Some say you are Elijah."

"I heard someone say you must be one of the Prophets of old."

The suggestion that irked Peter the most was the one offered by someone who shall remain nameless, who suggested that Jesus was in fact John the Baptist. To his mind that was just stupid, as the two men had been seen together at the same time, in the same place, so how could they be the same person? Ridiculous! Other suggestions were offered.

"Honestly...!" Peter sighed out loud to himself as he recalled the discussion.

But as unprepared as they were for that first question, the one that followed cut to the heart of the matter for all of them. When Jesus asked them, "Who do you say that I am?" they could no longer hide behind the foolishness of "others". A confession of their own belief was now called for.

There was a pause. There was no more smirking at other peoples' misunderstandings and foolishness. A light breeze gently caressed the leaves above them, exciting the dance of light and shade on the ground about them. Their own understanding was asked for. Their own foolishness would have to be brought out into the open for others to consider. Everyone fell silent... "Everyone except for me," thought Peter ruefully. "I have never been one for keeping silent," he reproached himself. If only he had been content to sit and watch the random patterns of sunlight, but that was not him. He always felt the need to fill the awkward gaps in their discussions; to get out the one thing that now burned in his chest. As he listened to all the misguided interpretations being aired, Peter looked at Jesus and said somewhat tremulously, "You are the Messiah. The Son of the living God."

Peter remembered becoming aware of everyone's head turning towards him and them fixing their eyes on him. No one said anything. Then as one they all turned their heads back to look at Jesus, waiting for his response.

Peter's belief was out there now. His heart had been shown and he stood vulnerable before his peers, his contemporaries, his... judges. In all honesty he could not construct a sound theological argument to support this belief if someone chose to challenge him on it and so it just floated there, defenceless, exposed between them. He had shared what he'd had burning in his heart and now everyone knew what he believed, right or wrong. No one spoke. It was Jesus's turn. It had to be Jesus who spoke next. Only his response was valid. Necessary actually. Unspoken, everyone's question was, "Are you? Is Peter right? Is he being stupid again? Hasn't he just blasphemed?"

Jesus' eyes were fixed on Peter and he looked deeply moved, as if Peter had just given him something of inestimable worth. Something very personal and intimate, though no material thing had actually been exchanged between them. It seemed as though Peter had just honoured Jesus and it clearly touched him deeply.

As Peter lay in the upper room with his face turned towards the wall, he recalled Jesus speaking next and blessing him for his confession of who he was. Peter's eyes welled up with tears as he recalled the blessing. For once in his life it seemed he'd gotten it right. He'd also 'gotten it right' before anyone else had and he'd made this confession in front of everyone else. This was really unfamiliar territory for him, but he also welled up because he recalled with regret the shame he felt for what immediately followed this minor victory of his. Why couldn't they have just moved on from there without further discussion? But they didn't.

As they moved out of the pleasant tranquillity of the dappled shade and approached the bustling village, Jesus was recognised by the inhabitants and people started running about, spreading the news of the group's arrival. Children were often the first to come running out to greet them, calling and laughing, free as the swallows that circled and swooped above them catching flies. Running in circles chasing each other. The adults put aside whatever work preoccupied them, then also started to gather about the visitors in small groups. The small groups merged into one small crowd that now walled them in. The people from the village thus joined the throng that was travelling with Jesus and this, as so often happened, halted their progress before they could enter the village.

Jesus bent down and picked up one of the smaller children that had been grubbing about in the dirt. Laughing, he blessed the child and wiped dirt from its grimy face, then setting the child down again as it wriggled like a fish trying to get away from the stranger and run back to its mother's skirt, regretting being brave for a moment. Then he would repeat the same with another child who came too close, laughing each time he did so. But there were always one or two of the youngest children who seemed to possess an unspoken insight or a more innocent trust in this stranger, whereas the older children and most of the adults had learned to be cautious at first, waiting for a stranger to prove himself before trusting him. The little ones would remain standing next to him, holding Jesus' hands or hanging on to the edges of his garments, feeling no imminent danger requiring them to return to the safety of their mothers.

On this occasion Jesus started to talk to the crowd that had encircled them. He talked about how, when he got to Jerusalem, bad men were going to crucify him, and Peter remembered how the very notion that this could happen was ridiculous. But Jesus never said ridiculous things, so this shocked him and he resolved to stop this idea developing further.

He took Jesus by the arm and, upset by what had just been suggested, blurted what was twisting his heart, with all the authority and outrage he could muster. "Never! This will never happen to you!"

As Peter lay in that upstairs room it was all too apparent that this had now happened to Jesus, just as he said it would. Peter had also denied him, just as Jesus had said he would. He was always right, Peter so often wrong. How could he have ever aspired to become a disciple? The people back at home were right, weren't they? The reality of the crucifixion was far worse than his imaginings back then on the outskirts of that village. The bad men that took Jesus weren't just bad. They revelled in the evil they perpetrated and loved the humiliation they brought upon their victims.

On the outskirts of that village Peter was determined to stop the nonsense. Surely God blesses good men. Rewards holy men like Jesus, doesn't he? He doesn't kill those who follow his commands, who perform such wonderful miracles as Jesus did. Does he? Surely all those commandments were given for us to follow so we would enjoy a long, healthy and prosperous life, weren't they?

What had happened to the certainties of a holy life lived well before a gracious God?

Peter winced as he recalled Jesus' stinging rebuke: "Get behind me Satan. You do not have in mind the concerns of God, only the concerns of man!" Peter did not wince because Jesus was angry with him, or even because he felt he did not deserve it. Jesus did not seem angry, as much as upset. Peter winced, because he always winced when he had gotten something spectacularly wrong, as he had that day. He winced because he had once again very publically gotten it wrong, again. He didn't seem to fail privately as often as he failed publically. "Why do I keep on doing that?" he asked himself.

It was right after this that Jesus opened his address to the crowd that had gathered about him with the words, "Whoever wants to be my disciple must deny themselves and take up their cross and follow me…" Peter didn't remember much more than that as his personal pain drew him to the back of the crowd, away from the direction in which everyone was looking. He reflected how so many would only take those words of Jesus as being metaphorical, yet the pain of the last few days showed these words were meant to be taken literally for some, as well as perhaps metaphorically for others.

Eventually sleep came to Peter and pain left him, for now.

The day continued in the upper room with some popping out to attend to pressing matters, others coming back with snippets of news about what was happening outside.

WALKING TO BETHANY

When Peter awoke the room was lit by a number of small oil lamps. He had been asleep for most of the morning and intermittently throughout the afternoon and it was now starting to get dark outside as the Sabbath was drawing to a close. There were some others who seemed to have followed his lead and were also catching up on lost sleep around the edges of the room, or escaping the pain of loss by sleeping. There was some activity around the brazier which now, to Peter's interest, was being used to cook the evening meal. Mary was helping her sister with the preparations, but Lazarus was keen to get them both back across the valley to Bethany before it got much later. Peter said he would go with them because it wasn't safe outside and John said he would go, too. There was still a disquiet about the city and all knew that since he himself had been raised from the dead, Lazarus was singled out by the Chief Priests as one who also needed to be "removed", as so many had put their faith in Jesus on account of his testimony.

After gathering their few things and receiving quick blessings from the other believers for a safe journey back, the five of them stepped out into the cool of the early evening. They took a similar route out of the city to that which Peter had taken into the city earlier that morning, avoiding the more direct route via the steps that ran adjacent to the house of Caiaphas. Retracing his steps they navigated their way through the back alleys to the gate that led them out of the city on to the road that took them back to the Mount of Olives and Bethany. The alleyways were busier now that the Sabbath was drawing to a close and their progress was slower than they wanted as they had to squeeze past crowds of travellers who had come to the city to celebrate the Passover and were milling about in unfamiliar surroundings. They had to queue to squeeze past one family of pilgrims who, like them, had come to Jerusalem to celebrate the Passover festival, but unlike them had nowhere to stay within the city. They were pushing an overloaded hand cart filled with the paraphernalia of their life on the road, trying to push and pull it down streets barely wide enough to walk two abreast.

It wasn't until the five eventually emerged outside the city walls that they started to relax, no longer spooked by shadowy figures in doorways; they started to feel as though they could talk freely. Up until that point their only communication made was out of necessity and in the case of Peter and John, in low tones in case anyone recognised their northern accents, which could have given them away. They spoke only to make sure they stayed together because from time to time it was necessary to move through the narrow allies in single file, so a "wait up!" was hissed so those up front would wait for those at the back, who had gotten held up behind other travellers also making their way into and out of the city. On one occasion the owners of the hand cart that had got it stuck in a hole and it toppled over spilling its contents into the damp filth of the alley floor. The ensuing delay became uncomfortable while each item was picked out of the dirt, wiped "clean" and reloaded on to the cart, before it could be slowly moved on again. Other than that, communication was limited to highlighting areas to avoid on the streets that no one wanted to inadvertently step in due to the poor light. It wasn't so much that what they had to share was secret or even that they were being subversive, but Peter's and John's thick regional accent might have drawn unwanted attention to them at a time when they wanted to blend into the melange of unidentifiable and unremarkable pilgrims.

Once they were outside and on the open road the group walked at an easier, more relaxed pace. No longer preoccupied with squeezing past or stepping over obstacles, they were now able to take the opportunity of a rare moment alone together to enjoy each other's company, rather than hurrying on to their destination. Previously when they had met, they had always had Jesus in their midst and their focal point. Even on the occasions when either Peter or John had spent time with Lazarus or his sisters, there were always others around that they had travelled down with, in particular Jesus, for whom their house had always been open. Peter and John had always been beneficiaries of their generous hospitality because of their association with Jesus, not because of any fame or celebrity status of their own. The door to the house at Bethany had first been opened to them because of Jesus. Would it still be? The question had not actually formed in their minds, but this rare moment for the five to be alone together seemed to highlight the new relationship they would now have, or perhaps would not have given that their common bond was now dead. The silence between them highlighted the difference that now existed in their shared circumstances. Lazarus was aware of the awkward uncertainty that threatened to come between them. They were all vulnerable and he wanted to remove any doubt that could undermine the relationship he himself held dear and could possibly cause them to become distant.

"Brothers…" he started, suddenly uncertain whether their minds were actually where he'd imagined them to be. "Brothers," he repeated and turned to look at Peter and John to make sure he had their attention. "I want to assure you that our house is your house. Our table is your table. For as long as we live you will be welcome to eat at our table and sleep under our roof. For I know he would have it no other way and neither would I. You will honour our house with your presence."

The sisters were glad their brother had made such a pledge and it served to reassure the two Galileans and cement their new relationship on the foundation of the old, making it a continuation of the same, rather than anything completely new, uncertain or awkward. Peter and John thanked Lazarus, both in turn clasping his hands and embracing him in gratitude.

Geckoes had started to emerge from the cracks in walls to feed on hapless insects drawn to the occasional torch lights along the walls. As they walked on Mary asked her brother a question about what two of the men back at the house were discussing. The topic was the one thing they each carried, nailed to their hearts, cold and hard like a lead weight. Whether spoken about or carried silently it remained at the forefront of their minds such that when anyone spoke of it all were immediately on topic.

"Two of the men were arguing about how Jesus could have been the promised Messiah if the Romans had so easily put him to death before Israel had been restored," Mary repeated the parts of the heated conversation she'd overheard.

No one answered immediately. Each had their own questions; some articulated, some not.

They walked on, trying to find the answers in the dirt that they kicked up, or in the bushes at the side of the road, or in anything… anything that would lift the burden of the "why" questions pounding on the doors of their consciousness, demanding to be answered.

Lazarus broke the silence. "There will be many more questions asked about Messiah, for many years to come yet, I suspect. Some will say Jesus is…" he paused "… was Messiah." He paused again. Then at length he said, "I don't know sister…"

John, in a desire to help his friend, offered, "We have all got questions for which we need answers. Far more questions than answers." John was buying time. Not that he really needed to, but he wanted to mean what he was about to say. "You know, Jesus seldom did what people expected him to do. He seldom did what *we* expected him to," emphasising the "we" as there was an expectation that those closest to Jesus fully understood all he did and why he did it. "You remember last week when we all came down this road. Jesus on that colt and everyone heralding his arrival with shouts and praises. Some were likening him to Simon Maccabeus. The conquering Messiah. You will remember that we ended up in the temple and there was a tremendous sense of expectation among everyone. We all got caught up in it and just as we were thinking 'this is it!' Just as everyone thought this is the point when Jesus announces his kingship and starts the overthrow of the authorities, he turned around and went back to Bethany to eat his evening meal at your house Mary."

The others smiled remembering the incident.

"He did do just that, didn't he…" Peter reflected. "I can recall a time back home in Capernaum when everyone was out looking for him on a particular morning. I think they all wanted him to do something or other, I can't remember what now. We all went out looking for him and found him up in the hills. John, you'll remember…" Peter said, turning to John to verify what he was about to say. "We told him everyone was looking for him and it was as if that was enough to drive him off in the opposite direction. Not scared off so much, but it was as if he was following a lead only he could see and only he could sense the urgency of. It was like he'd spotted something on the opposite hilltop and went off after it before it disappeared, with us trailing behind in his wake."

The group walked on in silence for a time, each lost in their own thoughts, wrapping their memories about them like a cloak to ward off the chill of a second night without their beloved. The road turned eastward towards the Mount of Olives and Bethany. They walked on, hugging their memories and savouring their warmth.

Peter broke the silence. "I can't believe all he did and all he taught was meant to end with his death. Who has ever spoken like him before? When he spoke he made me come alive. I mean really alive. It's like I had never lived before I met him." Peter was talking to himself as much as to the others, but they nodded in the darkness and agreed with the sentiment of what he was saying.

Peter continued, "Just then," and he pointed back to the road they had just walked down, "When we were talking about him, I started to feel alive again. For the first time since this whole dreadful… thing happened. It stirs something in me. When we talk about him, what he did, it's like just the mention of his name lifts this weight I carry inside of me. It can't end this way. It just can't."

John snorted a suppressed laugh, wanting to ride this tiny wave of nostalgic joy as far as it would carry them and share one of his favourite incidents. "Do you remember that time when we were in Capernaum and he gave that talk about how he was the bread of heaven and how everyone started to get upset when he told them they would have to eat his flesh and drink his blood if they were to have any part in him?"

"That didn't go down too well, did it!" Peter laughed a little. It was the first time he'd laughed for a long time, or so it felt.

"What happened?" Mary asked.

"People started turning their backs on him and wandered off, horrified by what he was telling them to do! They all took it so literally that they thought he was advocating cannibalism, but rather than disabusing them of their stupid literal interpretation of what he was saying, he just kept on and on, talking about drinking his blood and eating his flesh! There was hardly anyone left by the time he'd finished talking."

"There's not many of us left now," Lazarus observed. "What do you think the future holds for you men?" It was an unfair question.

Peter didn't know and said as much, shrugging, letting the weight of the hopelessness of their situation fall back on to him once more. Like one suddenly remembering he had momentarily forgotten he is in serious trouble, actually condemned and the moment's distraction let him forget.

"You just said this can't die with him," Lazarus said

Peter, so familiar with getting things wrong on so many occasions, sniped back with, "Well it seems as though it might have." He threw that comment out into the cold air in the hope that someone would knock it down with some insight that would bring him the reassurance he needed. He apologised, realising they all needed that assurance, then tried to justify his remark with, "It's just that…" and then gave up. He just ached for their circumstances to be different.

"There has never been anyone like him before, nor could there be anyone like him again," Peter observed after a time

They started to walk up the Mount of Olives, towards Bethany as the evening grew darker. There was a finality and hopelessness about Peter's last comment that none had the strength to refute. They were all disciples of a man that had just been put to death. A man so full of life, vitality and insight. Utterly captivating yet seemingly offensive to some who refused to believe him. The opposition's overwhelming might seemed to have finally won the fight. The small group trudging up the hill were on the losing side and it was as unpleasant as it was unexpected.

With their backs to city and the enormous temple illuminated against the night sky behind them, they drew close to the low stone wall that encircled the garden where Peter had stayed the previous night, their conversation also bringing him closer to his point of disquiet.

Peter, as he often did, felt he needed to fill the silence. "I will fish again," Peter said in answer to Lazarus's earlier question about their future. "When I get back home."

John thought that's what he would probably end up doing too, but didn't like the finality of Peter's statement. It seemed to draw a line in the sand, or rather a circle around all that they had experienced whilst travelling and ministering with Jesus over the past few years.

"I can earn a good living at it," Peter continued before anyone voiced their opinion "I'm actually quite a good fisherman."

"Yes you are," John agreed. Then added "...now that I've taught you everything I know!" just to pick up on an ongoing private joke between them, which the pair often used to tease each other to establish themselves as the better fisherman. John punched Peter's shoulder playfully to remind him of that.

They walked on in silence before John asked, "Is that it then?"

"Is what, what?" asked Peter, knowing full well what John was asking.

"Is that it? Are we abandoning the work we have been doing? All that Rabbi Yeshua started and wanted us to share in?" The question was testy and deliberately so. "Was it good while it lasted, but now let's turn our backs on it and get back to a 'real life'?"

"John, you know as well as I do that we are an odd bunch, the most unlikely group of disciples any Rabbi has had the misfortune to try and disciple. Look at us!"

The events of the past couple of days gave weight to Peter's point. The disciples had not covered themselves in glory. John didn't respond, so Peter carried on. "We can't be disciples if the one discipling us is... isn't..., isn't able to disciple us anymore. And furthermore, who among all the rabbis that you know would be willing to take us on, and even if there was one found to be willing, whose teaching would you be willing to follow?"

"Brothers..." interjected Lazarus, trying to calm them and cool the heat of the argument a little, lest it escalated. "…you know full well that it is not uncommon for the disciple of a respected rabbi to take up his mantle after his death. You two, along with James, were closer to him than any of the others."

"What are you suggesting?" Peter asked, knowing exactly what Lazarus was suggesting. "None of us have had any training except that which we received from the Teacher himself."

"Who better to carry on the work then?"

"It's not just the teaching. What about the miracles…? That is preposterous", Peter spat. "Rabbi Peter!" and he laughed at the ridiculous notion. "Rabbi Peter… pleased to meet you," he said again in a more affected tone. "No. Sorry Lazarus, that's really not me I'm afraid. John? Fancy being a Rabbi?" Peter was being facetious now and knew it.

"Don't do that, Peter. I don't know about having students or discipling anyone, but I've seen you share your experiences with anyone who would ask you. Will you stop doing that now? Can you stop?

"Of course not… So long as…" Peter didn't finish that sentence "No more than you could John."

However, the thought of being a teacher or regarded as a Rabbi leading a group of believers terrified him. Being part of an inner circle with Jesus was undoubtedly a privileged place to find himself. There wasn't that much responsibility in being a number two or a number three, but to take on the mantle of leader, well that could leave one quite exposed. Decisions would be expected, direction and counsel would be sought, people would ask deep questions of faith that he himself struggled with and they would soon find him out to be the fraud Peter was frightened he might be. The group had not spoken for a while, so Peter filled the gap with, "I know nothing but that which Jesus said and did in my presence… and how to catch fish."

They walked on a little further with just the soft scrunching sound of packed stones under leather sandal accompanying them. They wrapped their hands into the edges of their cloaks and wrapped themselves tightly to keep out the chill and the uncertainty of what lay ahead.

It was Mary who broke the silence. "Peter, you have a good heart," she paused. "Sorry, I don't want to embarrass you, and please forgive me if this comes across as too familiar, but just as the Lord himself was a strong man, his hands and body toughened by his life of labour as much as study, his heart was full of compassion, his love overwhelming. I think you have more in common with him than you are prepared to admit."

"She speaks the truth," said another voice in the gathering darkness. It was Martha.

"She is right," said John

"You have a humble heart," said Mary

Both women had been letting the men lead the conversation up to this point, but felt too strongly about the subject to let protocol have its way. Anyway, contrary to tradition Jesus had encouraged the women to take part in these discussions and on occasion publically praising Mary for being brave enough to cross cultural boundaries.

"You have always been the first to follow the Lord," said John "and in a sense that's what is needed now."

"Even when it meant stepping out of that boat and into the waves," said Lazarus with a smile that could be heard in the darkness. "Isn't that right, John?"

"Would you tell us that story again, Peter?" Mary asked. "I cannot believe you actually did that!"

There was a pause before Peter said, "What was I thinking? What idiot would think, even for a moment, that he could possibly walk on water?"

Privately Peter cherished this event more than almost any other because it was the one thing, the one event only he had in common with Jesus that no one else had. It was not something that could be learnt or taught. It was a moment that he had seized without thinking. Now forever immortalised.

"But you did do it," said John.

"Hardly," countered Peter, trying to down play any notion of an achievement on his part.

John started the story for Peter. "The Lord invited him to step out and join him in the impossible... and you did exactly that!" John had turned from telling the story to Mary Martha and Lazarus to telling it back to Peter, for his benefit as much as the others. "It was only when you started to look to yourself that you started to sink into the waves."

"Isn't that what you're doing now? You're looking at yourself rather than at him and starting to sink, Peter?"

There was another pause, then Mary asked Peter, "What was it like to step out of the boat and on to water?"

"Wet," Peter said, trying to justify the foolishness he felt and to diffuse the argument they were putting together, which was making him feel uncomfortable.

John said, "Yes, you did get wet in the end, but not at first. Tell us again, what was it like?"

"I don't know... it just seemed the right thing to do. The Lord told me to come to him and I did. It seemed simultaneously an utterly ridiculous and yet a perfectly reasonable thing to do because he was doing it and wanted me to join him. On reflection, I was more conscious of him there than what the water was doing beneath my feet."

Rather than being given the story from beginning to end, they had to tease it out of Peter piece by reluctant piece. "Why were you in a boat?"

"Where had you been?"

"Who else was with you?"

"Where was Jesus?"

"Why wasn't he with you in the boat?" On and on went the questions until all the details had been heard again.

"So much of his ministry seems to be like that," John finally added. "Utterly impossible, but perfectly reasonable, given who he is… or was…"

They concurred.

"This stuff just can't die with him," said Lazarus. "I don't see how anyone can keep hidden what you men have been through. All that you've seen and heard."

The exertion of walking up the steepest part of the road that led to the top of the Mount of Olives made their conversation a little more stilted. It was easier to think about what had been said than to talk more. As the incline eased towards the top of the hill, so their conversation resumed.

"What do you propose Peter?" said Lazarus "Who is perfect among us? Who among us could possibly fill Jesus' shoes, so to speak? Who is equal to the task? I promise you, I could not follow anyone who believed they had the necessary skills and attributes to continue the ministry the Lord started. Who knows where that person would lead us and I'm sure they would ultimately undo everything the Lord has been building."

They walked on towards the twinkling lights that could now be seen in and around some of the houses of Bethany. As they approached the home of Mary, Martha and Lazarus they thanked Peter and John for accompanying them on their journey. They invited the pair of them in for some refreshment before they turned back towards the city. The two accepted a drink of water and were about to head back towards the city saying they didn't want to leave the others any longer than was necessary.

As they turned to leave, Lazarus embraced them both and promised to meet up the following day. Following her brother's prompt Martha promised to bring over some more provisions for the group, for which the men both thanked her.

Lazarus said, "Remember his final words to us. He promised never to leave us, never to forsake us. None of what happened yesterday would have been a surprise to him. As much as we hated to hear it, he did tell us all this had to happen. My dear brothers, I have no idea how this is going to turn out, but he never let us down while he was with us. He never promised one thing and did another. Look at me." Lazarus wanted to emphasise his point "Who has ever done the works he did? I was dead four days and he brought me back! Who knows what wonders God is yet to work? I just don't see his ministry dying with him… I just don't."

Mary, Martha and Lazarus blessed Peter and John then prayed for them, this time asking the Lord to encourage them all in the work He still had for them to do, and to once again keep the men safe on their journey back into the city.

As they headed back towards the road that would take them down the hill towards the Kidron Valley once more, Peter and John walked on in the comfort of silence only good friends can enjoy, each lost in his own thoughts.

"I can't believe it's only a week since we followed him down this road, him riding that donkey…" John reminisced, after a while. "It seemed then that the whole world had finally woken up to his true identity: not just Jesus the man, the son of a carpenter from Nazareth."

"What happened? How can a people change their allegiance so dramatically in such a short period of time?" Peter asked, not really expecting John to reply.

"I don't know that they did," said John "They weren't the same crowd outside Pilate's residence baying for his blood. I was there. I know."

"You were?" Peter was surprised.

"His mother wanted to be near him throughout the whole dreadful affair. She wouldn't be dissuaded. I couldn't leave her so I resolved to stay with her, as did a couple of the other women.

"I should have stood by Him, John. I shouldn't have left you, but something came over me. I just couldn't bear to hear what was going on in the High Priest's house. What those men were doing to him." The shame that held the knife in Peter's stomach gave it another twist whenever he thought about his obvious weakness and not being there with John and Mary.

"Peter, I wouldn't have wanted anyone to witness what we saw yesterday. Such cruelty and such... such..." John struggled for words to adequately capture what he'd seen. "...such evil. Not just the killing of a good, innocent man, a holy man; but to revel in and enjoy every bit of the pain being inflicted upon him. Enjoying his humiliation. It wasn't simply evil. It was perverse. You wouldn't do it to a dog, much less a man. It's better you remember what he did for others rather than for what others did to him."

The night suddenly seemed colder as they walked back down the hill. The cloud that had been present all day had started to break up and stars were now visible between the clouds which were edged with a silvery ermine from the moonlight. The pale stone of the road they were on took on a luminescence in the dark, which helped them avoid potholes which would have caused them to stumble, but the shadows beyond the edges of the road started to play on their imaginations, concealing imagined threats that weren't really there.

They walked on down the sloping road until they arrived back at the low wall surrounding the Garden of Gethsemane again. Peter guided John towards the garden's entrance and said we need to pop in here briefly. There was a muted clank of a goat's bell from the far side of the garden as Claudia looked up on hearing their voices. She sniffed the air and recognised the smell of the inedible bundle that had ousted her from her shelter the previous night. Concerned that she once again faced competition for her bedding, she trotted back to her shelter and laid her claim to the dirty straw and ruminated whilst keeping a careful eye on these two shadows.

BACK IN GETHSEMANE

"So, why are we in here again?" asked John, looking around the grove that they had often met in with Jesus to spend some time away from the busyness of the city for prayer. Once it felt like a holy place, a place where you could commune with God easily, feel close to him. Its proximity to the temple across the valley probably helped with this. Now all that had been sullied by Judas's treachery... where *was* he now...? The garden's juxtaposition to the temple which loomed large across the Kidron valley from where they now stood had in some way added to the sense that it was a special place, a holy place. Now though, it felt like the temple owned it, like it owned and controlled so much that went on in and around the city.

"I spent last night here," Peter's voice broke the silence and interrupted John's thoughts. "I came back yesterday to look for the swords we discarded during the scuffle with the arresting party. I think they belonged to Ahaz. I'm sure they would have cost a lot and I didn't want them to be picked up by anyone else. I thought we should return them as we'd only intended to borrow them for the evening."

They walked towards the far edge of the garden, close to where Jesus had spent his last moments with the disciples before they were scattered like leaves driven before a storm. Peter started tentatively probing the shadowy undergrowth with his foot. Worried that he might disturb something in there that would bite him, he was stamping his right foot as he extended it, making more noise than strictly necessary as he searched the scrub where he thought he'd hidden the items. Eventually, just as he was beginning to think he'd left it too late and someone else had stumbled across them there was a dull, muffled metallic clank. He'd found them.

On the Thursday evening, as the arresting party arrived to capture their prey, three of Jesus's disciples, Peter, James and John, had been sitting close to him while he prayed. The majority of the party were sat nearer the entrance to the garden. As the three of them had sat there under an old olive tree, their intention was to join with him in prayer as Jesus had asked them to, one last time. Aware from what Jesus had been telling them over supper that this was their last night together, they prayed some sincere and heartfelt prayers; though unlike Jesus', their prayers were aimed at changing God's will, rather than surrendering to it.

"Please don't take him away, not tonight. Please don't take him away Lord, not now. Look at how much good he's doing. Look at how the sick are healed. Look at how the poor and the helpless have been given hope. Look at the love he shows everyone. Look at how he is exposing the hypocrites in the temple for what they really are! There has never been anyone like him before in all of Israel. He is your promised Saviour, please don't let the authorities take him away. Protect him Lord, from their evil plans… don't let the devil win… send your angels to save him…" and so on, until they ran out of words to pray and sadness and the hopelessness of the situation finally overwhelmed them.

Just what Jesus meant when he said he was going to his Father was still beyond their understanding. Or rather they didn't want to understand what he meant by it, as the literal interpretation of what he was saying was too painful to contemplate.

As Jesus characteristically surrendered in prayer to His Father's will, the disciples eventually surrendered to the heaviness which was upon their hearts and their eyes became heavy and they succumbed to the sleep their depressed state needed.

Twice Jesus came back to wake them, urging them to pray with him. Embarrassed by his evident weakness and lack of stamina for this kind of thing, Peter tried in vain to stay awake, pinching and twisting his hands uncomfortably to bring some degree of wakefulness, but the self-induced pain never reached his eyes, which convinced him it would be okay if they just stayed shut – even if other parts of him were hurting and awake.

Both he and John had been in possession of the swords Jesus had asked them to bring with them, which they only later understood was to fulfil what had been written about him being "numbered with the transgressors". This fact was not appreciated by Peter or John at the time. The initial novelty of carrying these weapons in their belts as they had headed out to Gethsemane on that night, soon wore off as they sat there watching Jesus pray. When Jesus returned a second time to wake them, Peter tried to prevent himself falling asleep again by playing with the sword he'd been given. Sticking it into the stony soil between his feet. Poking it into an old olive root and twisting the blade to see how far in it would go and how easy it was to cause the wood to splinter by twisting the blade. He checked the length of the blade and tested how securely the handle was fastened to it. He felt the weight of it and gently waved it about to feel the balance of it as it swung through the air. Nothing that any other red blooded male wouldn't have done in the same situation, given the opportunity to play with a weapon like this. John was no less a man and he too carried the sword because he was asked to, but he wasn't so easily distracted by fantasising about it.

Through all of history boys have dreamt of being brave, vanquishing soldiers, heroically defeating enemies in the face of insurmountable odds. Most of us only get to play with sticks to act out these duels with friends, but to be entrusted with a real sword, a real weapon, suddenly captures the imagination and feeds the desire to conquer your foe. For defending what is right, for protecting all those who are dear to you. For eliminating evil from the face of the earth. All this we imagine to be possible with the right weapon in our hands. This has never changed, regardless of the age in which we grow up. Only the weapons change and with them the extent to which good or evil can be effected in the lives of a few, or many.

The sword was still in Peter's hand when the arresting party eventually arrived to take Jesus away. Whether it was the culmination of his own sense of impotence and the frustration he felt as it became clear that his prayers were not to be answered, or the imminent departure of his beloved friend and saviour. Or maybe it was the shock at seeing Judas leading the arresting party straight to Jesus, seemingly betraying everything they held sacred, making a sham of all the prayers they'd prayed together, the worship songs they'd sung together, the good news they'd preached, the love and fellowship they'd enjoyed and even the food they'd shared. Maybe it was the gleeful look on the face of the sycophantic Malchus, the High Priest's contemptible, odious servant and his disrespectful tone in which he addressed Jesus. But when they started to manhandle Jesus, Peter lost his temper in an instant, saw red, and was compelled to force his way between this mob and Jesus. He had to intervene to stop this. It was wrong and just could not be allowed to continue, not while he was able to stop it. Malchus probably received the blow to the side of his head both because of who he was and because he had a manner about him which drew this reaction out of most people who encountered him. Good people who were never given to violence felt the urge to punch Malchus, just because of the disdainful look he always bore, basted in and perfected in a life full of his own self-importance, seasoned with self-seeking ambition and pride, which oozed out of every oily pore when you encountered him. Peter had actually aimed to take his head clean from his shoulders with one swipe of his sword, but as strong as Peter was, he was not trained in the art of close hand to hand combat so his clumsy, well telegraphed and poorly aimed strike hit the side of that nasty face, only severing the ear, rather than the whole unpleasant head. As startling as the outcome of this brief scuffle was, the reaction of Jesus to this show of violence was even more startling. Malchus's high pitched whiney yelp momentarily distracted one of Jesus' captors, who loosened his grip on his arm as he craned his neck over his captive to see what had happened.

This allowed Jesus to reach out to Malchus and touch his dangling ear to effect an immediate and profound healing. In the midst of the tumultuous scene, the focus of their hate, the very prey himself reached out in a characteristic act of grace and healed his attacker. That moment brought a temporary cooling to the temper of the mob and Jesus's arm was once again retrieved by his captor and pointlessly bound behind his back, as if to prevent him carrying out any further unwanted acts of grace. Curiously, an act that would continue in some parts of the church for centuries to come, managing more effectively with words and traditions than this soldier's rope, to restrain the Divine Healer, Jesus. For the time being though, the attention was drawn to the healed Malchus, who, believing he was mortally wounded, still held the side of his head with bloodied fingers, waiting for darkness to take him away. Then, as it dawned on him that even darkness didn't want him and checking that his head had been completely reunited with its ear, he cautiously resumed his mission to arrest this dangerous reprobate and march back with his captured prey to receive the praise and affirmation of Caiaphas that he longed for.

The momentary diversion of Malchus's ear being detached and then reunited with its head allowed John to get between the equally shocked Peter and Malchus. He relieved Peter of his sword and pushed him away from the middle of the crowd that surrounded Jesus. The severing of the ear, with the sudden gush of blood and Jesus' sharp rebuke startled Peter, who, stunned by his own actions, limply allowed John to disarm him. Once Peter and anyone within his immediate vicinity was out of mortal danger, John quickly withdrew to the edge of the garden and threw the two swords into the scrub that grew along the wall. He then returned to the edge of the crowd, which had started to lead their captive back out of the garden and towards the city with murderous threats to those of Jesus' followers, still in the garden who were calling out to him and trying to reach him. There were a couple of scuffles on the periphery of the crowd and one young lad called Mark must have said something that upset one of the arresting party. This caused him to be chased into the darkness. His pursuer grabbed at him and managed to get a fistful of his clothing. He started to pull Mark back, but to his credit, Mark bent over, twisted and reversed out of his garment and vaulted naked over the wall into the safety of the night. His pursuer threw the garment into the dust with a curse and shouted into the darkness exactly what he was going to do to Mark when he next saw him. Mark's pursuer, now irritated and frustrated, returned to the party empty-handed and angrily vented his frustration on Jesus.

The mob moved off out of the garden, back down the road from whence they came, back towards the city and the expectant Caiaphas, who was pregnant with dark deeds, intent on effecting his cruel revenge upon the carpenter's son who had become an embarrassment to him and a threat to the reputation he'd worked so hard to build up.

"Here we are," said Peter, as he bent down to retrieve the bundle he'd been looking for. Much earlier the previous day, as dawn had broken, Peter had found himself once more in the garden. There were signs of Thursday night's scuffle: a discarded lantern, a broken sandal, Mark's garment, and after a little searching, both the swords. Peter retrieved both, wrapped them in the linen garment and hid them from view in the undergrowth.

Peter brought the bundle to John saying, "We should return these to Ahaz."

"I don't know" said John. "What if we get caught carrying them back into the city?"

"The watchmen at the gate won't be interested," countered Peter "There are so many travellers milling around at this time of year that they will not check everyone. We'll just choose the right moment to re-enter the city with another group of pilgrims."

The two friends headed back across the valley toward the city to find their fellow disciples, who would naturally start to become concerned for their safety if they took too long returning. This concern for their fellow disciples once again brought to the fore the issue of who was to be their shepherd leader and they returned to the matter Lazarus had brought up earlier.

It was true. Jesus had forewarned them about everything that was going to happen to him, but they did not want to listen because the thought of it was too painful. They now wished they had listened more attentively. How it all needed to happen to fulfil what the prophets of old had written about Messiah. They had no doubt Jesus was the Son of God; he was the promised Messiah. He just wasn't the kind of Messiah most people had been expecting since childhood. He wasn't the vanquishing warrior so many in Israel had anticipated, or wanted. It wasn't just a saviour they sought; they craved revenge on those who held them captive not to forgive them.

The past three years with Jesus showed them he was so much more than the vanquishing warrior… but he was now dead and they didn't know where that left them. They felt isolated and overwhelmed by the loss of their beloved Jesus and the thought of life without him. Like a ship without a rudder, they did not know which direction the next wind of change would drive them. This was completely out of their hands now, which was probably the best thing for the future of the fledgling church.

As they approached the city gate there was a small group of travellers being allowed in. Peter and John followed them through with a brief nod of acknowledgement to the guard, who had let them out a couple of hours earlier. No one took any notice of the bundle Peter was carrying and Peter made every effort to not let the blades clank as he passed them. Any attention drawn to that bundle would not be welcome and would be difficult for an innocent pilgrim to explain away.

They made their way back through the narrow streets of the old city to the room, where the remainder of the group were staying. The poorly fitting, sun-weathered wooden door popped and waggled open once their identity had been quickly established and they were welcomed in by relieved faces who insisted they sat down and had something to eat. Once they had seated themselves they were handed small terracotta bowls containing boiled lentils, lightly spiced with cumin and garlic and a fresh loaf of lightly scorched flat bread with which to eat it. They gave thanks then hungrily tore off pieces of bread and dipped them into the hot runny stew, scooping up satisfying mouthfuls which left small globs on beards and moustaches as they were devoured.

MINISTRY AND THE STORM

S aturday night in the upper room passed at different speeds for those staying there. Some slept intermittently, others weren't so fortunate. The room was warm and quite crowded now; whispered conversations mingled with the sounds of those managing to snatch some much needed sleep. Some just curled up on their mats, resigned to the fact they were unable to sleep, and others didn't even attempt it. Some preferring to sit, staring into the sooty yellow lamp light; lost to their own thoughts.

Notwithstanding Jesus' repeated warnings about the events that would unfold once he'd reached Jerusalem, most could not have imagined they would have taken the form they did, or with the intensity of emotion and savagery that they did. The cruel treatment of the one who had never raised a violent hand to anyone, who only taught a life of love for God and for your neighbour, would be considered fundamentally wrong in any culture and wholly unwarranted. This Jesus of whom it would one day be written that every knee would bow and acknowledge him as Lord of all, let his drunken captors degrade and humiliate him. Yet, consistent with everything he taught, Jesus extended forgiveness to them through the searing pain they inflicted upon him.

It was these images playing over and over in the minds of those who'd witnessed them that kept sleep from them, their minds working overtime as they lay in silence.

"Why? Why did it have to be such a humiliating death?"

"Why such public shaming?"

"Wasn't there another way? Anything other than this would have been better."

"Where was God in all of this?"

By the early hours of the morning most had eventually succumbed to sleep. The few lamps left burning gave out a sickly oily light until one by one they guttered and failed. Around the room, one by one, hope had guttered and failed in the hearts of the disciples and darkness settled in the room as sleep finally granted them their moment without pain that they craved.

Before the first blood red streaks of Sunday morning appeared over the Mount of Olives another minor earthquake struck in the vicinity of Jerusalem. This went largely unnoticed by those that lived there, certainly by most of those who were sleeping in the upper room. Four of the women who had been sleeping in the adjoining room roused and headed out silently into the street below, each with a fragrant bundle in her arms. Hope may have been extinguished, but not their sense of loyalty and duty to their Lord. If they had discussed their plans with the men they would have been dissuaded from carrying them out because of the immediate, but as yet unquantified, danger they would be putting themselves in.

Love and loyalty were always highly valued by Jesus, as were simple acts of extravagant worship, and they knew he would have accepted this gift. It was their last chance to express their love for him in a practical way. Properly anointing his body for burial, a final dignifying act would, at least for these women, in some way redeem some of the humiliation he had suffered in death and the undignified, hurried burial he was given late on Friday.

As they made their way to the tomb no one took any interest in them, except for a few soldiers on early watch who, to relieve their boredom and to impress one another, made inappropriate remarks about the women as they hurried past, heads bowed, not making eye contact. Though the women did not understand what the soldier said, the men's laughter behind them unnerved the women and brought home the reality of their vulnerability. But this was the cost they had been prepared to pay for not involving the men in this venture.

As they approached the tomb where they had seen Jesus laid on Friday, their pace slowed as they picked their way through the garden to the tomb's entrance. Their uncertainty about how the stone was to be moved gave way to horror at the sight that lay before them. It seemed as though the tomb had been tampered with as the stone had already been rolled away from the entrance. Gasps of despair escaped from their lips.

"Oh no look... has he not suffered enough?" Mary Magdalen spoke to herself as much as to her companions. The four of them laid down their bundles on the damp ground and tentatively approached the tomb. No one wanted to be the first to look inside. If Jesus' body was still there it would be a distinctly unpleasant task washing and anointing his shredded skin, but a task they had mentally prepared themselves for. But if his body was not there... well, they had not expected his body to have been taken before they'd had a chance to prepare it properly. Eventually Mary was the first to approach the entrance to the tomb. Placing her left hand tentatively on the cold stone, she stooped and peered into the comparative gloom of the interior of the tomb, her own body eclipsing what little light spilled in through the low opening, making it harder to see as she peered in through the door.

The first attempts at daylight slipped into the room through open shutters to where the disciples were sleeping and one or two started to stir with their characteristic rough, early morning coughs and thoughts about stepping out to relieve themselves, or to get a drink of water, to lay the dust in their throats that had accumulated from another night spent sleeping on the floor.

Peter drifted in and out of sleep, consciously determined not to think about their immediate situation or what the future held for a disciple of a dead Rabbi. These thoughts, if given his full attention, would jar him awake as surely as someone shaking a broken limb. They exhausted him and he could do with more sleep to gain the energy he needed to face them once more. Had he been suffering from a broken limb, it might have been easier to sleep, but when it's the heart that's broken, it takes longer to heal and sleep often the harder to find.

Peter chose not to see if John was still sleeping. Instead he kept his eyes shut and attempted some mental exercises, hoping for just a few more minutes of peaceful oblivion. He set his mind to thinking about fishing and in his half sleep he pushed his mind back to Galilee, to happier days. The happiest days were when he and the others were working alongside Jesus. He remembered one occasion being out on the lake in his old boat; after a day in the stifling heat the weathered wood of the boat radiating the sun's heat back at him like an oven. They had been listening to the Lord teach and watching how he ministered to the crowd that had swarmed around him. He and some of the others would then attempt to mimic what Jesus did, with some or other effect. It was not something that he felt came naturally to him. Others seemed to move with a certain ease when it came to healings and deliverances. Others seemed to grasp the essence of the parables more quickly than he did. In fact, it occurred to Peter in one of his more sober, wakeful moments, that there wasn't an aspect of this work that he felt he really excelled at more than any of the other disciples. Choosing to avoid that recurring problem of doubt for Peter, he chose to return to his sleepier state of mind and recalled being back at the oars in the middle of his old boat. He secretly enjoyed watching the others climb in clumsily, trying to step between the irregularly spaced strengthening ribs of the hull, some as big as a man's arm. Trying not to slip in all the slime that coagulated there and the pools of water that had to be regularly scooped out of the boat to stop them from becoming too big. Peter smiled to himself as he watched those who did not fish trying to balance and not fall out or tip the boat as they failed to get into or out of the boat with any degree of dignity. He was much more "at home" on boats than most of the others, knowing automatically which way to turn his feet so they fit between the boat's ribbing, which had been worn smooth by his and his brother's feet over the years. It was second nature for him to step between the ribs, able to steady himself as the boat rocked and nodded in agreement with the unruly waters beneath it. The rocking and nodding, which seemed to affect some with a sickness that he had never suffered. Peter could row harder and row longer than others could. He could navigate with ease in daylight or at night. He could stay out on the sea longer, knew where and when to catch the best fish and when not to even attempt to go fishing. He knew how to keep his boat seaworthy long after others had allowed theirs to deteriorate unnecessarily through neglect or ignorance. He knew how to repair nets and sails, hook lines and all the skills necessary to succeed as a fisherman on the Sea of Galilee.

This particular day that came to mind he remembered vividly, as many of the others did too. The heat had been fierce all day and the land seemed to be breathing a communal sigh of relief as the sun finally slipped behind the western hills. Jesus was one of the last to get into the boat and exhausted from his day's work, he lay down on a cushion in the stern of the boat. He fell asleep almost immediately, they were barely twenty metres from the shore when his eyes had shut.

In his half dreaming, half waking state, Peter could feel the smoothed handle of the oar that had come to feel so much a part of him; a natural extension to his own flesh and blood. He could remember it was Andrew who sat beside him that day manning the oar corresponding to Peter's on the other side of the boat. He remembered pulling hard at the oar, setting the pace for the others to follow, to move away from the shore into deeper water. No verbal communication was necessary between Peter and his brother as they had done this hundreds, if not thousands of times before. He could hear the sound of the water slapping against the sides of this old boat as each stroke propelled them back towards home. He remembered the pale tangerine-tinged clouds hugging the hilltops to the east and the wind that started to pick up. He remembered how he had to strain against the wind to make any headway. He knew what it would take to get across to the other shore before the weather worsened. Ordinarily he might not have ventured out on such an evening as this with the threat of bad weather looming, but the ministry had taken longer than expected because the need was always greater than expected. The water was now slapping against the boat as the wind picked up.

Jesus slept. As Peter lay on his mat in the upper room he could see him now curled up as he often was. Utterly spent.

Everyone in the boat was dog tired, but not one person mentioned it. None were more tired than Jesus. Wrung out from giving out all day long, Jesus more than anyone slept the peaceful sleep of the righteous in the face of a growing storm, content that the day had been spent well.

They rowed on… the water now thumping the boat and crashing back into the sea. The old boat, lurching against the threatening wind, creaking as they strained harder.

Peter knew every inch of his boat. He knew where every creak emanated from and what each meant. He could feel the old oars creaking as they strained.

His back creaked and his legs ached. Still they rowed…

As the sky darkened the once emerald green water darkened with it, turning oily and threatening. It started to join them in the boat, crashing in over the sides. The water pressed in on them from every side, jostled them, just as the crowds had done all that day, crowds of humanity washing over them. Swamping them. Jesus' arms and head just visible in the midst of it all, as if swimming through the throng of people. He swam among them, through them, to them, rescuing them. They never overwhelmed him. Never drowned him.

As wave after wave of need crashed into Him, he met it, smiling, welcoming it with love and compassion. From the edge, Peter watched him, as if from the shore of the sea, watching him swim where he himself would have drowned. He felt sure he would drown.

Watching Him heal.

Calming the waves.

Meeting the need.

Showing the Way.

But now the man slept and they rowed on. Their turn to navigate the waters, there had been times when Peter wondered (unfairly, as he would one day realise) if this was the only reason he'd been asked to join the group; to help with the transportation needs.

They strained at the oars but could make no headway. As with the elements of this ministry, it occurred to him, "I strain but make no headway."

The wind was against them and growing stronger, the sky ever darker. They strained and grew weaker as the storm grew stronger. Once in the distance, it was now upon them and they strained with all their might, but they grew weaker still.

Yet Jesus slept.

They started to take on more water and the boat grew heavier as they grew weaker.

They were losing this battle. Sinking.

They prayed as they strained, their straining now going heavenward.

They were afraid.

They prayed.

They grew more afraid.

They prayed louder.

Jesus woke. And He answered their cry.

The storm submits. Recedes. Surrenders and retreats.

The once unruly water becoming calm, content once more to leave them now where they sat, no longer straining at the oars, but straining to comprehend what they had just witnessed.

Awe struck.

Who is this that commanded the storm, calmed the waves and met our needs? The question was unnecessary for they knew the answer. No man, but God alone could do such things.

There was no movement in the boat as all eyes watched Jesus return to his cushion in the stern and without another word, he curled up, bringing his knees up to his chest and fell asleep once more. The incident seemingly as insignificant to him as if he had just shooed a bothersome fly from his food.

Quietly they picked up their rhythm once more and rowed on… this time with ease.

Peter was now fully awake, staring at the rafters lit by the early light of the new day creeping in through the open shutters. "Who was He that on the one hand could do things like that in the presence of a select few, yet on the other hand allowed drunken oafs to humiliate him so in public?"

Peter didn't want to get up, preferring instead to lay there and think about the most vivid memory he'd just relived. It felt like the experience took on new significance for him now, on this morning. But he could not articulate why… and didn't feel he needed to. Well, not yet anyway.

Peter and some of the others had lived through that particular incident and many other miraculous experiences with Jesus that defied description, but this one, this memory, touched his heart right now. It was one of those miracles that only a few of them were privy to, which confirmed in his mind that Jesus was no ordinary prophet, but Messiah, the Son of God. Right now there seemed to be parallels with his current situation, his straining against a more powerful foe: his own doubt. He needed Jesus with him right now to calm the storm inside of him.

Jesus ministered with such grace and authority compared to his own clumsy and seemingly powerless efforts. The way the Lord dealt with the waves of need that crashed over him again and again; welcoming them and loving them. Peter was not sure he could do it. He was more certain he would drown under it.

Jesus did not seem to be subject to the laws of nature in the same way he was, yet… and the memory of it stung Peter afresh this morning… He lay dead and cold in a tomb a few minutes' walk from here. This brought Peter back to his senses again and the pang of the unanswered question, "What does the future hold for the disciple of a cold dead Rabbi?"

THE RACE

Peter's reflections and meditations in the relative calm of the early morning were brought to an abrupt halt with the sudden arrival of four distressed women, who seemed to care not that they woke the entire room with their tears and angst. Their breathlessness as they burst through the door did nothing to improve the clarity of the message they were trying to convey.

Their usual modest and neatly worn attire looked a little awry, giving them a slightly bedraggled appearance. The scarves that covered their heads had become loose and had worked back from their faces as they had been running through the streets, allowing loose hair to escape from its covering. The ends of the scarves were now being used to wipe fresh tears from their faces as their emotions bubbled over.

For these women, the trip to the tomb brought back the stark reality of the finality of what had happened to Jesus. Part of the purpose of their trip was so they could mourn properly with the body of Jesus, but the absence of his body brought to the surface a turbulent mix of emotions as they ran back past the now mildly-amused group of soldiers. They worked their way back through the old city streets to the upper room, where the men would now be getting up to start the day. In their confusion over the misplaced body they got lost as they rushed back through the network of small alleyways and footpaths. Shortcuts taken in one direction were now completely foreign to them in their distress as they tried to hurry back by the same route. Not being residents of

Jerusalem meant intersections of alleyways and roads, once barely familiar, all now seemed the same as they tried to navigate back to the others with the terrible news they bore.

As the women burst through the door the warm fug of unwashed bodies and smoke from the now expended lamps inside the room contrasted with the crisp, fresh morning air outside. Their noisy entrance had everyone's attention immediately, but because of their breathlessness from the run, the flight of stairs they'd just ascended and their raw emotions, it took several minutes to get a clear picture of what had happened. This was made more difficult because the men who'd remained behind hadn't appreciated that the women had gone out to the tomb. It was still early in the morning and the women's minds were working much quicker than the recently woken men, whose minds, like their hair and general dishevelled appearances, were not in good order, having just dragged themselves off of their mats. The group struggled to make sense of the garbled accounts given by the four women simultaneously.

"…the tomb was open…" they kept repeating, wailing "…there was no body there…"

"…the soldiers were there… well not there, but nearby…"

"…but he wasn't there…"

"Where?"

"…in the tomb…"

"…we took spices, but had to leave them there…"

"There were soldiers in the tomb?" someone asked incredulously.

"No!"

"Who wasn't there?" others asked, trying to get some clarity.

"Rabbi… Jesus… there was no body there…"

"What do you mean there was nobody there?"

"No! No… *body*, there!" Mary exaggerated a pause between the words 'no' and 'body'. "They must have taken it away for some reason," she said.

When Peter and John finally understood what the women were saying, they looked at each other. John's expression was a quizzical one, but Peter's was one of rage, which concerned John.

Peter shot back to the mat where he had been lying and quickly tied his sandals. John could see Peter's intention and did likewise, trying to slow Peter up.

"Wait a minute, Peter. Wait for me. What do you think has happened?" He repeatedly tried, unsuccessfully, to engage Peter to try and slow him up.

Peter wasn't going to wait. Grabbing his outer garment in his fist he ran to the door, flung it open and ran out down the steps without looking back. John, hard on his heals, called back to those still in the room: "Please wait here and keep the door shut while we're gone. It's not safe for us all to go…" and with that the two men were out of sight.

Peter had a good 100 metre head start on his pursuer by the time John had reached the street.

"Peter! Wait!" he called after his friend. Thankfully the streets were still fairly empty as they ran through them. Skipping over puddles and patches of filth, hopping round bored animals tethered to market stalls, where a few early tradesmen had just started setting up ready for business. The two men tore through the streets.

Peter wasn't a natural runner and the pace at which he set off, fuelled by the fury he felt at the thought of the Romans wanting to put the Lord's body back on display, started to decrease as the levels of adrenaline in his blood diminished. He felt this was something that would be so typical of those barbaric heathen pigs. Visions of his Lord's body once again being publicly humiliated flashed before his eyes and this drove him on as fast as his feet would take him. But as the exertion started to consume the adrenaline that had initially surged through his veins at the start, he slowed to a more sustainable speed. This allowed John to catch up with his friend.

For all the dark images that filled Peter's head as he ran, John's was filled with a continuation of the images he'd had just prior to waking. Possibly prompted by something Lazarus had said the night before as they walked back to Bethany, or simply from being in that man's company, but John had been recalling the various resurrections he had been a witness to while being with Jesus… There had been Lazarus's own miracle of course, but there was also the Centurion's servant back in Capernaum, Jairus's daughter and that poor woman's lad in Nain. There is no question that the Lord had dealt with death before. Healed it if you will. As if it was some sort of disease that had to yield to his command for life to return to the body. But how could he *do* this to himself, when he himself was dead? Could it be done, when he the One with the demonstrable authority over death was himself the one that was dead, as if in the end he'd finally succumbed to the unbeatable foe he'd defeated so often? Nobody had seen anyone open the eyes of someone born blind before, but this sort of miracle had become almost commonplace around Jesus. Similarly, not since the great prophets of old had the country seen the dead raised and again John had the impression that, given more time, this too could have become common place around Jesus… If only there had been more time…

As John and Peter ran on, Peter's head was a mess of anger and revenge, but it started to occur to John that Jesus had told them that after three days he would rise again. They had not really given much thought to what he was talking about at the time, because for him to "rise" he had first to "die", and that was where their thinking always faltered. Now as he ran it struck John like a lightning bolt. A glorious lightning bolt!

"Peter!" John cried from just a few meters behind his friend, as the two of them ran past the same group of soldiers that the women had just previously run past, twice. The soldiers thought about stopping these two fleet footed and evidently agitated men, but their watch would be over shortly and there was something in the eyes of the man in front as he ran past them fixing them with a stare and gritted teeth that suggested he wouldn't be easy to stop. In fact attempting to might cause them some personal inconvenience, if not to say injury. So they let the two run past unhindered. They didn't appear to be armed after all.

John called out again, breathless from the exertion, "Peter! I think he's done it!"

"What!" Peter shouted back breathlessly over his shoulder, not wanting a conversation right now.

"I think he's done what he said he was going to do!" John said, his excitement growing.

Peter didn't reply, but the excitement John now felt flooding through his veins removed all sense of fatigue and it occurred to him now that Peter was actually running unnecessarily slowly, so John increased his stride and glided past him effortlessly, now running with a smile on his face that came from a hope that he couldn't yet justify, as it had only just begun to be born in him.

Peter looked sideways at his young friend as John ran past him. Seeing the smile changed Peter's grimace to a look of sudden confusion and his pace slowed further as they reached the garden.

John ran through the garden, hopping and skipping over the rough terrain, straight up to the open tomb and leaned on the rock face by the opening and breathlessly peered in. He couldn't see a body, but waited for his eyes to properly adjust to the shadowy interior, just in case they were deceiving him and Jesus' body was actually still lying there... But no... he was not there. Just then Peter arrived and went straight into the tomb, nudging John aside without a word, but shooting the same puzzled expression at him as he had when John had run past him.

"He's gone, Peter," John said calmly though breathing heavily, his heart thumping in his ears from the excitement of the moment as much as from the run. "Like he said he would… It's the 'third day' today Peter."

John followed Peter into the tomb and squatted down on his haunches in the first chamber with his back to the cold stone wall and looked at his friend, who sat on the empty ledge in the burial chamber on the opposite side to the ledge where Jesus' body had been laid. He was staring at the bloodied linen strips that had once covered the tortured remains of his Lord, but there was no body. As the two of them tried to catch their breath they stared in silence, trying to take in what they saw before them, or more precisely what they didn't see, hardly daring to believe.

Looking at each other, John not able to stop smiling, Peter, now starting to sweat profusely from his early morning exertion, was still quizzical, trying to solve the simple equation, but not knowing where to start. This doesn't happen. This has never happened before.

The cold stone cooled the sweat that had formed on John's back and it now felt clammy and his clothes stuck to him.

"So you don't think we need to go looking to find where the Romans might have hung his body then, John?" Peter finally asked his friend. "… and what if you're wrong?"

"No… I don't think there's any need to… I mean, no… he's not dead. Not anymore…" It sounded crazy to John as he said it out loud. "This is like it was with Lazarus, Peter. Except the grave clothes are still here. He's risen… like he said he would be… resurrected. Oh wow, Peter!" John's excitement grew the more he thought about what he was a witness to. Then holding his head in his hands, he slid down the rough stone and sat on the floor, with his elbows on his knees, the palms of his hands pushing his dark curly hair up, away from his face. This action stretched the skin of his forehead, raising his eyebrows, which give him an even more surprised look than he had just previously.

After a minute or two he struggled back to his feet. As much as he wanted to stay there and stare at the empty grave clothes, John had an overwhelming urge to run back and tell the others, "Peter, we have to tell the others!" and with that the pair of them headed off back into the city. John with a bounce in his step and an occasional "Hallelujah!" and "Oh yes!" aimed at the sky. Peter, tired from his earlier exertions, tried to keep pace with his now very excited friend and limped and hopped along behind him.

It was now Peter's turn to try and slow his friend up. "Hang on John... please, wait... What are you actually going tell them? Slow up please! I think I've done something to one of my calf muscles... ouch..!" Peter tried to slow John up, not because he was badly injured, although something in his muscle had popped, which gave him an irregular and awkward movement, but he was trying to grasp the enormity of the consequences of this development... if they were right. But nothing was going to distract John now, not even his friend's discomfort, so Peter continued to hop, skip and limp as best he could behind his friend.

The previously twice bemused group of soldiers now got a wholly unexpected "Good morning men!" from one happy, previously agitated Hebrew that had come hurtling past them not ten minutes earlier. The one who did not seem at all friendly a moment ago seemed to have calmed down now and even said something as he hopped and limped past them... something about injuring himself whilst running? Peter tried to excuse his unusual appearance, lest they mistook him for a simpleton.

Anyway, the now thrice bemused soldiers looked at each other, shook their heads and all agreed they would never understand these people. They also determined their early shift had to be over by now and decided to head back to the praetorium because there was something quite peculiar in the air this morning, and who knew what was going to happen next? Whatever it was, they did not want any part of it.

What actually happened next was in one sense utterly insignificant, if observed impartially and objectively. In another sense it was monumental. Life-changing. Certainly it was for Mary Magdalene and all those who would believe in her testimony. It happened in the quiet of the now deserted garden, free from the wail of upset women and the noise and energy of excitable men. The tranquillity which returned was almost tangible. Mary Magdalene stood between the garden's winepress and the empty tomb, quiet but anxious. Ignoring the men's request that everyone stay in the upper room, she had followed them back to the garden, but at a much slower pace. Arriving there alone she remained at a slight distance until the men had turned and headed back to the city, shouting to each other. The men's excitable, noisy departure prevented them from noticing Mary and contrasted starkly with the peaceful stillness that now returned to the garden once more, settling as quietly as the dew had earlier that morning.

Mary, still believing someone had taken her Lord's body, sat on the large cold stone, which had previously been used to seal the tomb, staring at the exposed entrance alone, unobserved but feeling foolish and insignificant. The pain and loss she felt were hers to carry. The loss of the one man who had uniquely loved her as no other man could, more as a mother loves a daughter. He loved her for all that she was and wanted to be, not for what she could do or who she was raised to become. Other men had loved her, but they had loved her because of how she looked and how she moved, her grace and her smile. They had loved how she made them feel when they were in her presence, but Jesus was never like that. Ever since meeting the man, this man without equal, he had shown her what true acceptance was, what forgiveness was, absolving her of all the guilt she carried, for all that she'd done and had failed to do in her life. Her life had changed utterly because of him. Well, it *had*. Now she sat staring at an empty tomb. He was gone and she could not even mourn over what remained of his dead body because that had gone, too.

Her all-too-brief moment of mourning was interrupted by the arrival of someone behind her. The sound of twigs cracking under foot caused her to turn and look over her shoulder to see who was approaching. Seeing who she thought was the gardener walking towards her, she suddenly felt vulnerable and alone. Conspicuous because of her tears and that she shouldn't be sitting uninvited in someone else's property, she decided to take the initiative and asked if he knew where the body was so that she could go and retrieve it.

The 'gardener' looked at her and after a second's pause said simply and tenderly, "Mary."

That word 'Mary' was all that 'happened' next, actually spoken to the woman by Jesus himself rather than the gardener she perceived him to be. This woman, who for centuries to come would have questions raised about her personal history, about her reputation, her morality. The victim of ignorant scandal mongers who, being unable to conceive of the purity of innocent loyal devotion, would weave a fabric of rumours about Mary's relationship with Jesus in an attempt to taint the purity of the moment. Mary rose to her feet in an instant as she heard her name spoken in that all-so-familiar voice. Her hands clasped over her mouth as she jumped up in shocked surprise and she spun around to face him.

The moment the word reached her ears, her heart sang. It actually did more than just sing; it started a glorious song in her that would never die. It could never die. The word uttered softly and reassuringly, with his characteristic, uncultured northern accent, could not have been sweeter if it was sung by the hosts of heaven. It caused her heart to swell instantly, to burst with joy. She spun immediately she recognised the voice of her Saviour, the way he had always spoken her name.

"Raboni!" she gasped through her fingers, as if gasping for air when on the verge of drowning, as one gasps when a loved one returns unexpectedly after being away from home for far too long and all hope has been lost of ever seeing him again.

She cried.

She cried in disbelief at what see saw before her, as she moved towards him; the hands that were clasped over her mouth moving to embrace him. Her love set free again. To live again. She ran the few steps to meet him and embraced him. Jesus, the object of her love restored. Pure love once more allowed to live and to be expressed. A purity known only by hearts touched by the love of God. Hearts that have remained untouched view such acts of intimacy with the distorted scepticism of love portrayed by perverse soppy tales of romance, or by suspicions of infidelities or improprieties.

Mary's heart had been touched by Jesus before this moment, set free to love and free to worship. It was said that Jesus had delivered her of seven unclean spirits; the nature of these and the outworking of their uncleanness in Mary would be the cause of the vile speculation about the type of woman Mary was. And herein is the problem in describing such a simple but intimate moment; the unhealthy obsession with speculating about the person's undisclosed past rather than their redeemed present and future changes what is perceived by the onlooker. The interpretation of the actions in the garden are dependent upon the perspective from which they are viewed.

Mary was a worshipper of God. An expressive, extravagant worshipper. One not satisfied with offering what others considered an appropriate act of devotion. She knew what was appropriate as evidenced in her adoration of Jesus at Simon the Pharisee's house during an evening meal the previous week. Led to anoint him for burial before he had even died would be an unusual act in any culture, but to pour out an entire alabastron of quality perfume, equivalent to a year's wage, was unprecedented. Her simple, true heart was honoured by Jesus and defended by him when she was criticised by others, even when despised for doing it by her fellow disciples. The critical comments shattered the moment for Mary, making her feel utterly foolish and profligate, feeling naked and vulnerable before men once again. For that moment there was no one else in that room, just Jesus and her, but the room suddenly became crowded with others and noisy with the criticisms levelled at her and the extravagance of her worship. Rather than being a beautiful, innocently extravagant act, it had been determined as excessive and frankly embarrassing. By all except Jesus, that is. The act was for him alone. No one had his permission to comment on it, yet they did.

Because of Jesus, Mary would be held up for all eternity as the acceptable standard of worship for God: extravagant, abandoned and selfless. A standard that would continue to draw criticism from those of lesser hearts and bigger purses.

Jesus met with Mary first that Sunday morning, honouring the woman who was not ashamed to honour Him in company that was deeply critical of her for doing so. Honouring the woman in a culture that did not; a culture which considered them to be second-class citizens. Not even trustworthy enough to bear testimony in a court of law. He deliberately entrusted this first resurrection appearance to one whose testimony would not normally be valued by men. The choice was now theirs to make. Would they allow themselves to believe her, or would they allow their culture to blind them?

SUNDAY - BROILED FISH

There are a number of things to be borne in mind when broiling fish:

One is to always oil both sides of a fillet, rubbing in your favourite herbs and spices. If you are broiling whole fish, the skin should be pricked with a skewer or cut with a knife to prevent it from curling and blistering. If broiling skin-on fillets, slash the skin a few times to prevent it shrinking and broil it with skin towards the source of heat.

Choosing the right fish and following the above principles should result in a tasty meal, according to Martha.

True to her word, Martha, accompanied by her sister Mary and brother Lazarus, travelled back into the city of Jerusalem again on that Sunday morning. This time they brought with them bread, which she and Mary had baked earlier that morning, plus some cakes of dates and raisins. They also brought their donkey, on which they placed a bag of grain and a mill stone, to help the group grind their own flour and bake bread as they had need. They tethered their donkey at the foot of the steps leading to the upper room, where it waited passively, ears drooped, staring at the dust beneath its feet, resigned to spending the rest of the day in the city. Martha stopped to negotiate the purchase of some large river fish from a vendor who she thought had inflated the price unreasonably, just because of the increase in demand for food from all the pilgrims in the city at this time. After settling on a price that neither party was happy with, Martha followed Lazarus the short distance across the street and up the steps to the room, he carrying the bread and cakes of fruit, Martha carrying the very expensive fish. Mary paused at the foot of the steps to kiss the donkey between his ears and told him to be a good boy. She then scratched his cheeks and ran up the steps after her brother and sister. When they reached the top they found the door to the room was locked shut, as it had been all the previous day. Lazarus juggled the two heavy bundles he was carrying to free a hand so he could knock and make their presence known. In the end he used his right foot to bang on the base of the door, trying not to lose his grip on the cargo he was carrying as it threatened to slip to the street below.

His identity was asked for and given, just as it had been when they'd arrived the day before. Notwithstanding the considerable care taken to keep the room as secure as they could, and the fugitives' presence within it secret from the outside world, once the three visitors entered the upper room, it was quite clear that there was a different atmosphere in the place. There was an unrest among the disciples, an agitation, a frustration, which threatened to spill out of the confines of the room. Mary, Martha and Lazarus had not expected this. Grieving was anticipated, mourning would have been normal, and this was the topic of their discussion that morning as they walked from Bethany to the city. They discussed how each of the group that were known to them would cope with the loss of Jesus. Who had whom to support them? Which of the group was most likely to find the shameful nature of Jesus' death the hardest to come to terms with, and if not cared for properly who was the most likely to wander away from the group?

All this that they were anticipating would fill the day they were about to spend with the group in the city, but the nature of the unrest and frustration they found was not anticipated. Once they had handed over their bundles of provisions to the women in the room, they were updated on the turn of events that had precipitated this unrest during the early hours of that morning.

The sharing of this news with the three new arrivals now instilled in them the same sense of unrest that pervaded the room. Lazarus now wanted to talk to Peter, John and Mary Magdalene to get the first hand reports because the second hand accounts they had just been given seemed confused and didn't make sense. It sounded like Jesus was no longer dead, like he had come back to life, and that couldn't be true. Could it? Even for Lazarus whom Jesus had himself brought back to life after being in the tomb for four days, this still sounded crazy to him. Would no one die anymore? Ever?

Peter, James, John and a handful of other believers were gathered at the far end of the room, some with their hands stretched out towards the rafters, others were on their knees, heads bowed. All seemed to be praying, some out loud, others rocking to and fro silently, but no less fervently than the noisy ones, just their lips moving so none but God could hear them. Lazarus and Mary moved across the room to join them. Mary sat nearby, listening to what was being prayed, whilst Lazarus stepped into the group, next to Peter. They were asking their Heavenly Father for wisdom, understanding and guidance on what this all meant. They were asking him to direct their next steps and as Mary sat within earshot she agreed in her heart with the requests being sent heavenward, believing the prayers to be Spirit born. Trying to apply the principles Jesus taught, she added the weight of her agreement to the prayers she understood. Lazarus did likewise, trying to catch up with the theme of what was being prayed. It is not always easy to join in on a conversation, or in this case, a focussed prayer time, when not fully appraised of the circumstances leading up to it.

Just what the men were seeking guidance and wisdom about was beyond the new arrivals' understanding initially, but as the time of prayer progressed it became apparent that God was doing something significant and as their understanding of the situation grew, Mary and Lazarus "amen-ed" at appropriate points. Mary resolved to be patient and wait until the praying concluded, when she hoped she would be able to learn more from the discussions afterwards.

After the prayers had been said there seemed to be more of a peace about the group. Grateful for this change in the atmosphere, the men kept their peace before engaging in conversations with their neighbours, not wishing to lose this tangible benefit, which they now felt. It was as if the act of simply praying and engaging God in their concerns brought about the resolution to the problems they were asking Him for; even if for the onlooker there did not appear to be any appreciable change in their circumstances. Maybe it was just the act of praying which engendered in them a renewed confidence, an expectation that God was about to do what they had been asking Him for, and this dispelled some of the angst they had previously felt. It has to be said that this was not a universal effect on the group. Whilst some remained quiet after the prayer time, their expressions showed they were unconvinced that their prayers were heard and they felt the burden they carried beforehand remained theirs to carry still.

After this time of quiet, Lazarus greeted Peter, who he had deliberately stood next to. The two men embraced and moved to a space to one side of the room. Peter could tell from Lazarus's expression that he was eager to know what had happened that morning, so Peter was happy to share his version of the events. Frustratingly for Mary, her brother, who didn't seem to appreciate she had been patiently sitting there waiting to listen in on their conversation, had taken Peter to the other side of the room. Undeterred, Mary stood up, crossed to where the other women were sitting and dipped two small jugs into a large jar of water and brought them to Peter and Lazarus. They thanked her and as they returned to their discussion she settled down nonchalantly by herself, but within earshot of the two men to glean all she could from their conversation. Her efforts were not in vain as others of the group started to congregate around Lazarus and Peter, adding points of detail they thought would help.

Peter told Lazarus that Mary Magdalene and some of the other women had risen early that morning and had gone out to the tomb in Joseph of Arimathea's garden to properly anoint Jesus' body. Then by way of adding commentary to Peter's account, John, who was sitting across the room talking to Martha, explained that his burial had to be done hastily on Friday because it was getting late by the time they had retrieved his body from the cross.

"Did none of you men go with the women?" Lazarus asked Peter, but looked around the faces of the group which now encircled them, unable to hide his obvious concern.

"No," said Peter, feeling a little defensive. "They hadn't told us what they intended to do and because they were sleeping in the other room, none of us heard them as they got ready and went out."

Lazarus tried to change his tone to reassure him. "Sorry. Please excuse the tone, but I was just concerned about them being out in the city at this time. Go on."

"Me too," said Peter. He then went on to describe Mary's and the other women's return to the group and his and John's subsequent sortie to verify their account of the empty tomb. Peter told Lazarus why he and John had run there immediately: that he was concerned the Romans had determined to put Jesus' body back on public display. He described what he saw when he entered the tomb: the blood-soaked linen strips left on the ledge within the tomb, where Jesus' body had been lain, but the absence of any body.

There was a long pause while Lazarus considered what Peter had just shared with him. There were a thousand questions to ask, all seeming to start with "But…"

"But how…?"

"But where..?"

Mary was also struggling to digest all she had heard, but it was she who was the next to speak, rather than her brother. Both men turned to look at her and the group surrounding them parted slightly, surprised that she had been sitting there listening to them – even more surprised that she felt she could be a part of their conversation.

"So you're confident it was the right tomb? Sorry, it's an obvious question, but could there have been a mistake?" Her challenge made the group turn their attention back to Peter.

"It was definitely the right tomb," John said. "The women saw him placed there on Friday and the bloodied linen cloth was the one Joseph and Nicodemus had used to wrap him in, to carry him there from the execution site."

There was another long pause as they each tried to figure out what had happened to the body. It was then that Peter told them about Mary's return to the garden and her claim that she had seen Jesus, but more than a simple sighting, Mary said she had spoken to him and he to her… and she had touched him! She claims that he is very much alive. As alive as he's ever been… Solid, not a spirit.

Then John, who had been updating Martha on the same events that Peter had been telling her brother about, came over and joined them. He looked excited. He was probably the only one in the room who did. He was actually having trouble containing his excitement. John then shared his version of the morning's events, which matched Peter's in every respect, except that he had to mention that he had outrun Peter and had got to the tomb first. As he said this he gave his friend a sideways glance and a smile, to which Peter just shook his head, as if in disbelief that John could consider this a pertinent point to make at such a time as this.

John then shared his belief that what had occurred this morning was exactly what Jesus had been teaching them about when he said that he would be raised again in three days! Lazarus and his sister both stared at him open mouthed, trying to absorb what he'd said, but neither of them said anything. Both Lazarus and Mary had quite a unique perspective on all this. Being the recipients of a personal miracle, perhaps more so in Lazarus's case than Mary's. They were acquainted with the pain of a delayed, but ultimately astonishing miracle at the hands of Jesus. Lazarus experiencing it first hand in suffering the illness which culminated in his death, and Mary witnessing this suffering as she tended to her brother during the final stages of his illness. Mary then witnessing Jesus raise her brother from the grave after he had been dead for days. It was a measure of the anointing on their Lord's life that he moved in such miraculous power, but that was different again to this situation. Jesus was alive when he had carried out that miracle. Now he was dead, or at least that was what they were certain of until a few minutes ago. Now their world was being turned upside down again by this man Jesus. From the first day they met him until the last, nothing was normal. Could this be true? If it was, what did it mean...?

"Where is Mary Magdalene now?" asked Lazarus.

"Well," said John, "When she came back, saying she'd seen the Lord, the women she had originally gone to the tomb with first thing this morning wanted to go back to see him, too."

"Have any of the men gone with them?" Lazarus interjected, not able to hide his concern for them again.

"Yes they have," said Peter "Andrew and three of the younger men have also gone with them."

"That's good," said a less anxious Lazarus. He then said, "My next question was going to be: "so what do we do now?" but I now understand why you were all seeking guidance in prayer earlier…" His question tapered off as he tried to digest what he'd heard already.

"What else can we do?" said Peter

And so their morning progressed in indecision with occasional bouts of prayer.

Around midday, the party that had ventured out to the garden where the tomb was returned to the group and a fervent chorus of, "Did you see him?;" and, "Was he there?" but after their rather deflating, disappointing response, there was an immediate anti-climax and a sad resignation of those who had been eagerly anticipating their return. For some it was a resignation to a further wait for a corroboration of Mary's sighting of the Lord, to confirm her assertion that the Lord was indeed risen from the dead. To others it was a resignation to the fact that Jesus was still dead. The fleeting glimmer of vain hope that he wasn't had disappeared like the morning mist, again thinking that clearly his body had just been misplaced or taken somewhere…

Two of the more disillusioned disciples, Cleopas and his wife, decided it was time for them to head back to their home in Emmaus. A couple of others followed their lead and said they should be getting back too. There was little desire to remain in the city to see out any more of this festival they had travelled to Jerusalem to celebrate, so it was that the disappointed parties started to gather their meagre belongings together, embraced other members of the group with heavy hearts and started to head out the door, not knowing when or if they would ever see each other again. The group had started to disintegrate. As disbelief extinguished the flame of hope in one it spread to another. Cold water being poured on the smallest of flames that had just started to gutter and die in their heart.

The day dragged on with little more being achieved. A further rumour reached the group that Judas Iscariot was dead. This brought another shock and another stab of pain and sadness to the group. They all knew it was Judas who had betrayed the Lord and in that sense they saw his error as responsible for Jesus' arrest and conviction. But Judas was one of them. He was one of "the twelve". They had travelled the length and breadth of the country ministering with him over the past three years. They had doubts about him naturally, but Jesus didn't seem to share their concerns. In fact when they had suggested that Judas might be helping himself to the group's money that he had been put in charge of, Jesus let him continue in that role, in full hope and expectation that his trust in him would help him to change his ways. Judas might have had his issues; they all did in different ways, but nobody wanted him dead. They first received the news from the family that owned the house they were staying in. Ahaz, the owner, who seemed to know everyone in every walk of life in the city, had heard it from one of his acquaintances who had found the man hanging from a tree on his land. When the group first heard of Judas's death, their heightened state of anxiety caused them to fear this was an indication of the start of a wave of persecution against them, which they had been expecting. But the man who had come to their door with this dreadful news tried to reassure them that as far as he could tell, Judas had hanged himself. It appeared to be suicide, not murder. Apparently Judas had been seen in the temple the previous day in quite an agitated state, ranting at the chief priests and apparently throwing money at them. By all accounts he looked very disturbed and dishevelled. Two of the men volunteered to retrieve the body of Judas and make sure he was respectfully buried.

"Why did Judas choose to betray the Lord and leave the group?" Mary asked in all innocence.

"I don't know what he was thinking," said Peter, utterly mystified by this turn of events. "What was he trying to achieve?" he asked, pitching his question to no one in particular, eventually concluding with "what is going on?" either as a question to himself or a prayer. It was hard to tell. All points of reference seemed to be in the process of being erased.

These were the saddest and strangest of days.

Lazarus decided to ride his donkey back to Bethany to retrieve the handful of disciples who had been sheltering there since the arrest of Jesus on the Thursday night. As the group had been scattered that night, five of them made their way to the home of Mary, Martha and Lazarus, who were happy for them to shelter there with them. They believed it to be safer for them to do this than to go back to the city. The city now held an unquantifiable threat for the followers of Jesus, and whilst the unquantifiable remained unquantified, it was agreed that given the day's turn of events it was important that all the disciples knew about the empty tomb and the sad news of Judas. They should be given the option of coming together or choosing to leave, as others had.

Lazarus returned some hours later with four of the men. Thomas preferred to stay where he was, choosing not to believe the nonsensical babblings that Jesus was alive. It was a level-headed and rational decision, one which no one could present any tangible evidence or logic to refute. He and everyone else in their day was well acquainted with the sight of dead bodies, particularly those who had suffered death at the hands of the Romans and their penchant for slowly despatching enemies of the state on a cross. Victims of this cruel apparatus took a long time to die, and they stayed dead.

Nevertheless the miracles they had seen while they were with Jesus were astonishing works, especially that of the raising of Lazarus. But these were miracles that had been worked through a Jesus that was alive and breathing. It was quite clear that there was not one among his followers that had any track record of raising the dead like Jesus had, so Thomas had therefore preferred to take the sensible and rational option and stayed behind in Bethany. It was the safer option and he wasn't going to give in to any hysterical nonsense.

Whenever the various and disparate groups of disciples met up, which often happened when the Galileans came to Jerusalem for the festivals, there was always a hunger to know what had happened since they had last been together. Each in turn would share the stories of their various escapades. This was particularly true when Jesus was ministering among them and it was true now that he wasn't. When the four men that travelled back with Lazarus arrived, they wanted to know every detail of that morning's events.

It was good to be back with the group, even if the dynamics of it were but a shadow of the one that had been gathered around Jesus on the Thursday evening before his arrest.

As the evening drew in, Martha's sister Mary gathered the various small clay lamps, which were dotted about the room, and placed them on a board by the door. She then descended the steps outside, carrying an empty dipping jug and an old alabastron and went into the home of the owners of the house. They were in deep conversation, so rather than interrupt she simply held the jug and alabastron aloft to show the purpose of her intrusion, and Esther pointed to the side room to her left where the large storage jar holding the oil was kept. Mary moved the cover to one side and dipped the small, black jug into the clear gold-green liquid. She removed it, letting the surplus oil drip from its shiny rounded base, before carefully pouring the contents into the slender alabastron. She repeated the action, dipping the small, jug back into the oil once more, allowed the surplus to drip back into the main storage jar, and topped up the alabastron. She then dipped the jug a third time back into the oil, filling it to the brim and after letting it drip for a minute, repositioned the cover on the large jar with her elbow, as her hands were full, and went back into the family room.

Smiling at Esther and mouthing a "Thank you", she walked to the door where Ahaz had been sitting. He stood and opened the door for her and let her out with a sympathetic paternal smile. Mary ascended the steps outside and gave the door at the top a gentle kick, being careful not to spill the precious oil and asked to be let in. Once inside the low light was starting to make the room really quite dark. Mary started by filling the lamps she had gathered on the board with the oil contained in the alabastron. It was easier to control the flow of oil from this than it was with the small dipping jug. When she had filled all the lamps, she recharged the alabastron with oil from the smaller jug. This would be used to top up the lamps so they would maintain their light as the night wore on. The wicks were trimmed and she lit each lamp with the taper she had lit from the brazier, which was being prepared for cooking the fish purchased that morning. The lighted lamps were carefully returned to the soot-stained niches around the room where they had previously resided. A large, grey, circular lamp with six wicks around its circumference was placed in the centre of the main table, but it would not be lit until they were ready to eat their meal.

Martha cut the fishes and rubbed them with oil and spices and placed them over the burning coals. Flour was ground, mixed with water, and the dough kneaded until it was smooth. Handfuls of the dough were flattened and baked into the flat, unleavened loaves they always ate as their staple food.

As they sat around the room to eat together, Peter led the group in prayer, giving sincere thanks for the food they had been given, using the words that Jesus had so often used to thank his heavenly Father as he broke bread with them. It was a precious, if somewhat sombre, moment as memories both tender and raw shook each of them. Some could only think of the happier times when Jesus was with them. Days they had never wanted to end. Days they never dreamed would end, certainly not the way they just had. Yet here they were: disciples without someone to disciple them. If they were honest, from that perspective, one could describe this as a pointless group, even though they shared an unparalleled history together. An unparalleled history that promised such a future. They had been so privileged to have lived with Jesus, seeing such incredible miracles through his ministry first hand. Receiving unique insight into his profound, yet simple, teaching, which those outside of their immediate group struggled to grasp. Each of his parables was like a point of light to navigate by in the inky darkness of this hostile and confusing world. The normal, everyday imagery He used to convey eternal truths remained with them. Whenever they saw farmers sowing seed or reaping they would remember the stories he would tell of the Kingdom of God. Whenever they would see workers in the vineyards a host of parables would come to mind of God's generosity, his patience and his desire for fruitfulness. They had also been the recipients of his unconditional love, forgiveness, grace and undeserved honour, yet they had also seen him turn on the Chief Priests, Scribes and their company, who expected to be honoured and revered, and issue them severe warnings about their blatant hypocrisy. What this group had shared with Jesus was too precious to have died with him, but no one had any clear idea of what the future held for them beyond the immediate pressing need to return home safely.

The fresh bread and broiled fish were placed on platters in front of them with an array of condiments and vegetables. They served each other in the manner that was customary for Jesus to do before they helped themselves. The bread and fish were well cooked and they were sincerely grateful for the food, but none had their usual characteristic appetites, each preoccupied with the recent events. Conversations were held in twos and threes around the room, each confiding in the other their hopes and fears, their expectations and doubt. Each trying to remember what it was that Jesus had told them about being handed over to sinful men who would kill him, then being raised again on the third day, and what that all actually meant now. Their hearts were heavy and so were the conversations and this fuelled their anxiety about their future as a group… as a church. Bowls containing cakes of dates and raisins were passed around the room to augment their meal.

While the meal was still in progress there was a sudden and unexpected gasp of shock from one corner of the room. Horror perhaps… then another gasp. Two of the women sitting on one side of the room with their backs to the wall; both had their hands clasped across their mouths staring directly ahead in disbelief. Motionless. The conversations stopped abruptly and everyone turned to look at those who had made the noise and were now sitting frozen, staring beyond those that were seated opposite them. Everyone then turned to see what it was they were looking at, and with that there were further gasps and men suddenly scrambling to their feet, as those in the room tried to figure out whether the person who had unexpectedly appeared in the room was friend or foe. Should they welcome the visitor or run for their lives? Food was dropped and drinks were knocked over as people clumsily and hurriedly got to their feet, jolting the board they sat around and everything set upon it.

After what seemed like an age, but was probably only a few seconds, Mary, the Mother of Jesus, spoke in the gentlest, but most certain of voices… "Son… !"

Her voice cut through the hiatus. It was her immediately recognisable voice, flute like, but with a slight quake from the emotion of moment.

It deserved the hiatus so that it could be heard in perfect clarity and not drowned in the hubbub of the mealtime conversations. Her lone monosyllabic exclamation brought forth a chorus of whispered questions from others in the room. The same question, just phrased differently: "Lord?"; "Rabbi?"; and "Is it you... is it him?" as other voices in the room joined his mother's. With the sudden chorus came a greater stirring among those assembled.

The light in the room was poor as the few oil lamps created large areas of shadow, which grew larger as people stood and eclipsed the meagre light still further. But as the visitor drew closer to the diners, they could see it was him... he was smiling broadly, on the verge of laughing even. It wasn't the laugh of one who had the satisfaction of surprising others, or of one who had duped another and their shock bringing his delight because he had outwitted them. Rather it was the laugh of pure joy, of one reunited with his family; joy bubbling over, the perfect antidote for the pain and separation they'd experienced in Gethsemane. His smile was the panacea, the remedy for all the failure, all the grief and the shared humiliation. Now they were reunited, with hope being re-born as the truth was revealed in the person of Jesus. The truth being realised corporately and individually.

"You are alive...?" was the whisper, hushed by the wonder of the moment, as each struggled to believe what they saw before them. No one dared breathe, lest it dispelled what they saw before them.

With the exception of two anxious souls, who terrified beyond any logical reasoning by the arrival of Jesus, attempted a hurried escape... once they had fretted over and finally managed to unlock the door, which for an awkward moment had everyone's attention because of the noise they made and for a time it looked like they were never going to master the latch, pushing rather than pulling in their blind panic to get out. Once they were gone, everyone in the room turned back to face Jesus and slowly gathered around him. None spoke, but each with a thousand questions on their lips. They just stared at him in wonder and disbelief. It was him. Jesus smiled at them and loved them. Some placed their hands on him, on an arm, or a shoulder, his hair, or his chest; whatever was within reach to reassure their other senses that what their eyes saw in front of them did actually exist and was not a figment of their imaginings. The group parted slightly in front of him to let the diminutive figure of his mother through. She stood before him and reached up a hand to tenderly cup his face as she'd so often done throughout her life, and she loved her dear son's face one more time. Now the most precious of all times. Jesus in turn covered her hand with his, looked at his mother and smiled, their eyes sharing the understanding they alone had. The room watched on in silence.

After a time, and as much to break the silence as to demonstrate to all in the room his alive-ness, Jesus asked, "Do you have anything to eat?"

There was plenty to eat. No one had been particularly hungry this evening.

Attempting to regain his composure, Peter said, "Erm… yes… of course… sorry…" as if struggling to decide how customary protocol should apply when the previously dead, now resurrected, come to visit. It was rude not to offer the guest at your meal something to eat, whether they were dead or alive… again. Peter turned back towards the table and retrieved a broad terracotta dish which contained some of the broiled fish and offered it to Jesus, dumbly wondering what Jesus was going to do with it.

Jesus looked at the fish and "Mmmm-ed" his approval. He thanked Peter and pinched some of the white flakes of flesh from the bones and popped it into his mouth and chewed as the group watched on in awed silence.

"Mmm, that is lovely," Jesus said appreciatively once he'd swallowed the mouthful. He said this specifically looking at Martha, whose cooking he recognised from the blend of spices she liked to use. She smiled, removing her hands from her mouth momentarily where they'd stayed ever since he'd entered the room so he could see her nervous acknowledgement of his compliment. She then lowered her eyes as tears started to well up again and her hands moved back to covering her mouth once more.

Jesus looked around at the group, who were utterly absorbed in the moment, transfixed by his eating. This made his smile broaden further, just as a street performer might surprise an already amazed audience by executing an even greater feat, or as a juggler might seek to amaze an audience by adding another item to an already implausible number of objects circling through his hands. So Jesus stretched out his hand and to the amazement of the crowd, whose eyes tracked the movement of his hand without blinking, took another piece of fish. With his eyes meeting theirs, he deftly popped it into his mouth and chewed, again to the crowd's astonishment, as if they'd never seen such a feat before. Then, because even when you're resurrected fish bones are an unwelcome inclusion in any mouthful, Jesus paused, put his fingers between his lips and retrieved a large fish bone, before swallowing his mouthful.

Needing to ease the tension that had grown in the room since his appearance, Jesus turned to Peter and asked if he had tried the fish, characteristically bringing the ordinary into the extraordinary. Peter confirmed he had, but as he was holding the dish, he took a piece and fed it through his copious facial hair and chewed on it, just as his Master had just done. Then, just as his master had done, he too paused while he retrieved a bone from his mouthful, before swallowing and nodding to indicate how agreeable the fish was. Next John, then James and Andrew all took pieces of fish from the dish, as Jesus took it from the frozen Peter and passed it in front of them – not because they were still hungry so much as they would take anything Jesus offered them, and this was how it always was… and how it always would be.

When the dish was empty, Jesus returned it to the table and looked at each of them saying, "See, it is me," and as if he could sense the disbelief in the room, he commented, "Look… look at the nail marks in my hands and look at my side… Here… where the soldier's spear went in." The disciples looked on in amazement.

Jesus, their Lord, was back among them. He bore the wounds from the injuries that had contributed to his death, but they troubled him no more. He was suffering no more. He was complete, he was healed, he was whole, but the marks remained as evidence of the price paid. The job done.

The thousand questions each disciple was carrying started to bubble out, but as was Jesus' custom he waited for these to die down because they were not relevant or important. Then he blessed them all. Looking at each one in the eye and loving them as he spoke, he said, "Peace be with you. *My* peace I give to you." Then he breathed on each of them. The gentle breeze of his breath seemed to pass through each of them, clearing away all residue of the anxiety and grief that they had been carrying for the past few days, making them feel alive once more. Invigorated even. More alive than ever before.

Then, as suddenly as he had appeared among them, he left them almost as if he dissolved into the shadows that existed between the yellow pools of light emitted by the lamps. Peter ran to the door and pulled it open to see if he could see Jesus outside in the dark to beg him not to leave just yet. Peter breathed into the darkness outside, "Just a few more minutes… please!"

John was at his back trying to look beyond him into the darkness, too. But Jesus wasn't there. He had gone. The two men turned and walked back into the room, pushing their way through the crowd of enquiring faces that had gathered at the door behind them. Closing the door, the disciples all stood looking at each other in utter amazement. Then those closest to her turned and embraced Jesus' Mother and wept with her and for her, because there are no words in any language that could adequately convey the sentiment or the emotion of the moment of his visit. John embraced her saying, "Mother…" affirming the new relationship Jesus had inaugurated as he hung dying. Peter, James, Andrew and the others started embracing each other excitedly, energised and invigorated, not really knowing what to say, or even what the crazy events of the day meant for them, but the fact that nothing like this had ever happened before in all of human history, and they were witnesses to it, had the most intoxicating effect on them. They started to laugh, nervously at first, then full blooded guffaws. These stopped suddenly, thinking they might have been inappropriate, given that Jesus' mother was in the room. They looked in her direction and apologised. She in turn raised her tear-streaked face to them and beamed a smile that brought more light into that room than a thousand oil lamps could have. Raising her hands and shrugging her shoulders to them, she signified it was perfectly okay to laugh, or cry, or jump up and down. Everything was appropriate on such a night as this!

MONDAY - RETURNING HOME

Jesus told his disciples he would be going back to Galilee ahead of them. The disciples needed no better invitation to pack up the few belongings they'd travelled with and cut short their sojourn in Jerusalem. They headed en-masse back on to the road that would take them back to their homes, families and the now promised company of their newly risen Messiah. They bade farewell to the Lord's friends Ahaz, Esther and his family, who had let them use the upstairs room for the past couple of weeks, promising to return if they could and if it was in God's will for them to do so. Nothing was ever to be taken for granted anymore.

As they headed out of Jerusalem, Mary, Martha and Lazarus accompanied them past their own house in Bethany and out to the edges of the village, and as was so characteristic of Martha, she had given the group heading back to Galilee enough bread, boiled eggs, pickled fish and dried fruit to sustain them for the first couple of days' journey. Lazarus had provided them with some money to cover any other needs they may have on the trip. Their goodbyes were emotional. The group had grown closer during the time spent together in the week leading up to the festival and especially during the past few days after the death of their Lord. Neither group wanted to leave the other, but circumstances were such that practical matters demanded their attention. Homes, businesses and livestock all willingly given up to follow Jesus now seemed to take on a new prominence in their thinking since his death. These would all need to be attended to, and even for those who had not given up everything to follow Jesus, this was the cost of pilgrimage for Jews able to make their ascent up to Jerusalem.

After committing one another to the Lord's care, Lazarus and his sisters stood in the road and watched their dear friends pick up the pace for their return journey northwards. A gentle breeze pushed at their backs, flapping their robes, as if urging them to re-join their friends, but they stood and watched in silence. They watched with arms around each other until the small, beleaguered band disappeared from view. They turned aside and returned to their own home with heavy hearts. Would their friends return to Jerusalem again? Why would they want to? And even if they did, would the whole group return, or just a few of them? The mission, their purpose for being, seemed in danger of crumbling apart now that their friends had left. There really wasn't much more they could do, other than to continue to pray for them.

For their part the pilgrims did not relish the thought of journeying back. The trip was always physically tiring and the dangers they faced until they reached home, both real and imagined, just added to the fatigue. In the past it was always a wrench to leave the spectacle of the City of God, the magnificence of the temple and all the pomp and holy ceremony that accompanied it. All that which had once drawn them on these pilgrimages now seemed to be driving them away. The spectacle had become the spectre. It was the religious leaders' determination to preserve the status quo, to stamp out anything that challenged their authority, or more specifically exposed their genuine lack of true authority, that had led to their connivance with Rome to murder Jesus. None of that spectacle would ever draw these Galileans back again. The tradition, which once was a joy and a comfort to the travellers, now held a naked, unveiled menace for them, which had probably always been there for anyone who, like Jesus, dared to challenge it. But this had been hidden from this small band of earnest believers, as it was from most earnest, trusting pilgrims.

Around midday, the group took a break from their walk, when the warmth of the day started to make their clothes stick to their backs and their hair stick to their faces, foreheads glistening with sweat. They sat by the side of the road in the cool of the shade offered by some leafy sycamore fig trees. Letting the gentle breeze minister to them, drying them and refreshing them. They sat for a while without speaking, each lost in his or her own thoughts. The usual banter and songs were not shared on this mornings' trip, so the time passed slowly and each step was an effort. There was too much to think about. Peter sat with John and the two men shared some fragments of the now dry bread, which Martha had prepared for them earlier that morning. Peter sat with his back to a tree and stared ahead without speaking as he slowly crunched some of the bread and took the shell off one of the boiled eggs, without looking at it.

The tireless, frenzied rasping of the Cicadas in the trees and bushes about them filled the silence that sat between them. Peter was staring across the road to a patch of long grass bleached almost white in the glare of the midday sun. The gentle breeze gusted from time to time and Peter watched the grass bend and jerk, with each gust passing through it. As his mind idled on this image he was trying to decide if the grass looked like it was clinging to the earth where it was rooted, tenaciously resisting the urging of the wind to break it free, or if the bending and jerking of the stalks was the grass's attempt to free itself of the roots which were holding it down, preventing it from flying free with the wind. There was stability and security in the rootedness of the grass, but there was excitement and adventure with the wind, wherever it was blowing. There were significant and powerful winds blowing through Peter's soul.

They weren't random, he knew that. God was driving them, but who knew where they were being driven or what was in store for them? Peter had choices: did he want to stay in Galilee, where there was some stability earning a familiar living from fishing the sea as he and his brother had done quite successfully for years before they'd met Jesus, or did he want to extract himself from that life and let God drive him on to who knew where? To be like the grass in the wind as it were; to break free and go with Him wherever He leads?

Peter's musings while he ate were interrupted when the view of the grass was obscured by another party of travellers arriving, wishing to avail themselves of the shade that the trees offered. When they had eventually organised themselves and arranged the clutter they carried in ordered heaps of blankets, pots and bags, they settled under the trees. The group's patriarch tethered their old donkey on the opposite side of the road from Peter and John. Peter watched the animal crop the stalks of grass he had been staring at, removing the hypothetical choices he had imagined were the grass's to make. The breeze gusted again, but the now shortened, ragged stalks no longer bent or jerked under its caress. They just stood there rooted to the spot, largely unaffected by the wind. The moment seemed tragic and snapped Peter from his reverie, but it had lodged an image in his mind that he knew he would ponder on further.

Impatient to get home, he stood and urged the others to restart their journey northwards, making the excuse to his companions that they should get going again and allow this other party of travellers to benefit from the shade they had been enjoying. With a few sighs and groans, they helped each other to their feet and picked their bundles, which always seemed to gain weight as they travelled. They each voiced their appreciation for the food Martha had given them and, refreshed, they headed back out into the bright sunlight to continue their journey home.

* * *

Nothing of significance seems to happen in villages. If it did, I suppose more people would be drawn to live in them and they would in time no longer be villages. Folk from towns and cities don't always appreciate the joy of simple rural life. Even family members who may have been away on a trip for just a few weeks forget that nothing much happens in their small, rural community. And when they return, an often asked question is, "So, tell me what has been happening while I have been away...?" And those that have remained behind have to scour their memories for something newsworthy, to avoid giving the immediate and obvious answer: "Nothing really", because it's the all too frequently used response that reminds the traveller why they went travelling in the first place. But to search for some piece of news that will match the fascinating tales of the traveller, who has returned with all sorts of experiences, is often a fruitless one. On the rare occasion that there is something fascinating to share, it has the potential to be socially awkward in case the news takes the sun off the traveller's tales. But seldom can those who live in villages compete with a traveller's tales; the painful banality of local news is best kept to the day to day exchanges between those in the community, who will better appreciate its minor significance. The traveller will usually hold court and enjoy a status of the more widely experienced of the immediate group around him – be it family, or old friends, or even just old acquaintances renewed. What villagers seldom value is the beauty of the simplicity of their life, compared to the apparent excitement of all that goes on in the bigger towns and cities. People return "home" to villages because there is a constancy within the simple life they offer. Travellers value this when they are away and will speak fondly of home with their new exciting companions. Yet when home they will speak of the exciting new acquaintances they have made, which in the ears of their audience seems to reinforce their perception of village life as a dull life. A life not spent well. A life not achieving. A life of little value to God or man.

When Jesus ministered in the northern territories of Judea, he went through all the towns and villages. His very presence, as well as the miracles he wrought, transformed these communities. People from all over the land came to see the place where these things that they'd heard of had happened. They wanted to meet the blind man who had received his sight at the touch of Jesus' hand. They wanted to meet the dead girl or the dead boy, now alive again. They wanted to see the stone pitchers that held the water he had turned into wine, or stand where he stood in Tabgha when he multiplied bread and fish for a poor and hungry crowd. For many years to come, crowds of similarly hungry travellers would continue to do so, travelling from village to village, being shown where the events took place by those that were there, or as the years passed, by the children and grandchildren of those that had been there.

As this band of travellers neared home, people came out to meet them and wanted them to stop and talk with them about their pilgrimage up to Jerusalem. They wanted to hear first-hand about the magnificence of the temple, the splendour and majesty of the City of God. They wanted to hear stories that they too could relate because if you are unable to travel yourself, the next best thing is to share the experiences of someone else who had. But the tales this band of travellers had to share ranged from the too painful to talk about, to the downright unbelievable. To talk of Jesus' arrest, execution and burial was excruciating enough, but the questions asked by the hearers would all too quickly highlight the disciples' desertion of Jesus at his greatest time of need. These were stories the travellers did not want to share, yet. The eyewitness accounts of Jesus' resurrection were the tales that burned within the disciples and the ones they wanted to share, but these were too often met with sideways sceptical glances or derisive laughter. "Who has ever heard of a man who has come back from the dead?" Even the simplest of village folk knew this didn't happen and their natural disbelief cheapened their most precious memories.

And so the effort of the journey was magnified and the eventual arrival home was a weary one. However, it was Mary's countenance that caused many who heard their tale to believe. Here was a mother who had not only lost her first born son, but had watched as he suffered the cruellest of deaths. Yet here she was comforted by the knowledge that he was not dead. She was not grieving in the way mothers do in the agony of a child's death; indeed the way so many of them had as they'd lost infants and adolescents to diseases and accidents. There was something in Mary's conviction that her son Jesus was alive, even though he was not counted among the group that had travelled back, which was unshakable.

The nearer the group got to home, the more the group fragmented as they took their respective paths that led to their homes and families. And so the eye witness accounts were spread as everyone wanted know what had happened. No detail was allowed to be left unsaid. Peter found the reliving of the arrest, his denial and the execution particularly hard to recount and quickly resolved to resume his trade as a fisherman. Something he knew he was good at and could do by himself or with the assistance of Andrew, James or John. It was more than just a way of putting food on the table and selling the surplus; it was about recovering all that he'd lost. He knew people questioned the wisdom of giving up his fishing business to follow that itinerant preacher. God had made some people scholarly and fit to be a Rabbi's disciple or a teacher of the law, and others he'd gifted with strong backs and arms to be fishermen, craftsmen and farmers. And Peter was conscious that he definitely, in their opinion at least, fell into the latter group. In time, Peter thought, he would regain through fishing the respect he was sure he'd lost by being characteristically over-enthusiastic and impetuous in giving up everything to follow Jesus. In time, as he once again started to bring to shore some of the larger catches of fish, people would start to respect him again as the capable fisherman he knew he was. Bringing in food for the community, he would once again become that immediately recognisable character in the region, for all the right reasons.

It was only a couple of days after arriving home that Peter invited James, John and some of the other disciples to go out on an all-night fishing expedition with him. They had done this before because it tended to reward them with the bigger hauls of fish as it was easier to catch the fish at night. Peter had spent the day out by the water's edge, just a short walk from his home in Capernaum. He had initially started checking his nets, taking his time doing what he had done for years, repairing any damage that would allow his precious prey to escape. He had also prepared the lamps needed for the night's activities, ensuring they were charged with oil and had sufficient wick to burn brightly all night. The boat was seaworthy and a few large and small baskets were optimistically placed on board. After the chores were done, he sat alone pensively, looking south across the shimmering sea, which reflected different hues as the sun traversed the sky throughout the day. Peter listened to the water gently licking the smooth stones along the shoreline and looked out across the sea as Egrets crisscrossed over the water's surface as if riding an invisible cushion – keeping them a hand's breadth from disaster, sometimes alone, sometimes in pairs or small flocks of four or five, but always with purpose. Their long, elegant necks curled back on themselves as they flew with such grace and apparent serenity.

The familiar sounds, smells and surroundings of home brought some comfort, but also conflict. Someone was singing in the town some way behind him and the voice was barely audible. He thought it was probably the newlywed couple who seemed to be blessed with some musical talent and were often heard singing love songs. She certainly had a beautiful voice and it drifted out through the trees to where he sat in his boat, unimpeded by the stillness of the day. The melody he could make out was a familiar one and the words she sung spoke of the eternality of love. Her joy was like a balm for the ache he felt, as he sat alone and listened.

There was an occasional distant clank from bells belonging to the small flock of adobe brown sheep on the hillside. Fleeces matted with dirt, the sheep grazed in the company of a handful of black goats on the hills to his immediate right, the sheep's ears flopping down the sides of their faces as they ate, like soft leather slippers. The three wiry young boys watching over the flocks negotiated rocks and the steep slopes with the same agility as the animals they were looking after, as if they were made of the same stuff. Once the flock had settled to graze on the still green grass and wild flowers, the boys set about practicing their skills with their sling shots. They were aiming at something obscured from his line of sight by the long grasses, but from their body language it was evident that the older boy was better with his sling than the two smaller boys. This was much to the older boy's amusement and their frustration. Inevitably, after a time, the teasing from the older boy elicited harsh words from one of the smaller boys and he moved away from the other two to sit alone, taking a renewed interest in the flock, which did not taunt him for his shortcomings.

The rolling Galilean hillsides that cradled the sea in their steadfast embrace were home to Peter. He could name families from every village you could see when you were out on the water. Some considered the place beautiful, but it was more familiar than remarkable to him. There were deep waters and places where rocks lurked dangerously close to the surface of the sea, places where you could shelter when a storm came upon you, and places where you were not welcome to go ashore. Granted, in summer when the grass turned a golden yellow it looked a most perfect setting for the beautiful blue green gem that is the Sea of Galilee, shining like a precious stone, polished and set by the Greatest Artisan of all. But right now, as Peter gazed out over the waters before him, he didn't just see his preferred areas to fish from. What he looked at around him were places that had been forever transformed by Jesus. This shallow inlet where he now sat had become the place where he had taken Jesus into his boat and pushed out a little from the shore and listened to him preach. The distant twinkling of lamps and firelights from S'fath seated high on the hillside above the sea, no longer were simply a navigation aid at night, but were now a reminder to him to "shine his light"… to be someone he wasn't by nature cut out to be. Peter sighed deeply and looked for an answer in the sky to the questions he couldn't even construct. Why did his head and heart ache so much?

Peter stood and stretched, realising he had been sitting in the same place for too long, then deftly stepping between the boat's ribbing, moved to the bow and hopped over the edge onto the stony beach. He walked from the water's edge and leant back against a smooth grey rock that protruded from the scrub that grew around the sea. He reached into the woven bag he had left on the rock and withdrew a couple of plump dried figs. He pulled the stalk off one and popped the whole leathery fruit into his mouth and chewed on it slowly, enjoying the rich, honey sweet taste of its crunchy, seeded interior. Peter looked down at his feet and saw a crack in the sandy soil beneath the rocks where a column of ants busied themselves, carrying bits of leaf and fragments of dead things to and from their nest. Having swallowed the first fruit, Peter took the second fig and held it by the stalk end. He placed its flesh between his strongest and most closely matching teeth and bit into the fruit's soft flesh. With a slight sawing action of his teeth, he bit through the fruit. He examined the remnant of the fig he held between his thumb and index finger, then he looked at the ants below him. Enjoying the taste of this fig more than the first one he'd just eaten, he decided to bite off a little more of the sweet, dark flesh before carefully dropping the rest into the path of the ants at his feet.

This is something he had liked to do as a child and he smiled as he remembered doing what he thought were benevolent acts when he was young. He also remembered stirring up some of these ants' nests and watching the frantic organised repair jobs the ants would embark upon. But today his gift of a sweet treat excited only a small number of ants as they experienced this unseasonal good fortune. He watched as they clambered excitedly over the chewed stump, tasting it, examining it, running away, then running back to examine it again, as if in disbelief that this should fall from the sky out of season. A few then set to work to bring it into the community, hurriedly scurrying about it, standing on it, pulling at it to bring parts of it into their home. The majority of the ants though ignored the fruit and continued about their own business of carrying impossibly large fragments of leaves and twigs with some or other objective in mind. It made Peter reflect on what he was watching… maybe, somehow… he was like God, Jesus like the fig, and humanity like the ants. But that was an imperfect picture because Jesus couldn't be a half-chewed fig… and God would undoubtedly have better teeth than Peter had… and He wouldn't have chewed the fig in half before giving it… people were like ants though, he thought. The majority were always too busy to notice God's gift to them.

Not far behind Peter was Tabgha, where Jesus had given each of them a small piece of fish and a ripped part of a loaf and told them to feed the thousands that had been with them all day. And in *his* hands the bread and fish increased as fast as he could give it out. The supply of food just never dried up; not until everyone had had their fill. Further along the hillside and a little higher up the slope was where Jesus had taught crowds how to live lives pleasing to God. Across the water he could see where Jesus had dealt so sovereignly with that terrifying individual at Gadarene. He could also see across to where Jesus had calmed the storm and where they'd seen him walking on water. And as Peter remembered, he looked at his feet, then back to the water, where he had woefully attempted to do just what Jesus had done that time, and walk on water himself. No one else he knew had ever... would ever have attempted such a thing. "Stupid," he muttered to himself, hating his failure.

Jesus had changed everything for him. Nothing he looked at was the same anymore, nor would it ever be again. What made it painful, the thing that drove him to sit out by himself today when he should have been attending to chores that had been left undone by his absence, was that Jesus was no longer with them. This light that came into their lives and burned so brightly had now gone and everything, every colour, every smell, every sound, was a muted tone of what he had made it while he was with them.

So Peter resolved to try and reclaim some of his former life by going fishing. Andrew, John and the others were equally keen and so as night started to fall, they pushed away from the shore with their net on board and lamps lit, tentatively resuming a familiar old task. But this night was different from all that had gone before. They caught nothing. They'd not even seen shadows of fish in the water below their lamps. Nothing. It was as if nature itself had turned its back on Peter and his companions. Peter had started to feel a bit like Jonah: a bad presence on board. He had started to convince himself that if he were not in the boat the others would have fared much better. Was there now a curse upon him? In his mind he had failed at being a loyal, effective disciple and now he was failing at the one thing he'd never questioned his ability to do: fishing. What else could he do? They'd had fruitless fishing trips before, but they were fatigued this morning and everything looked a little more bleak than it might have otherwise.

The fatigue from working all night exaggerated the feelings of despair that overtook them as they decided to head for shore. The dark sky had already started to turn a pale blue over the hills to their east and with it the advantage of night fishing started to slip away from them. Their motivations changed from catching fish to simply catching up on the sleep they'd lost in this fruitless pursuit. As they neared shore someone shouted to them to try casting their nets on the other side of the boat, but they were too tired to throw it out again. Their hands were sore from this exercise, which they'd repeated all night, to no avail. Their tough fishermen's hands had softened while they'd been away from their boats and they had lost some of their stamina for the night's work which had sustained them since boyhood. But the person on the shore was quite insistent and as they were headed to the part of the shoreline where this person was standing, they roused themselves one last time with, if they were truthful, some mild annoyance at having to cast their net into the sea with no expectation of catching anything.

They weren't prepared for the resistance the net gave when they tried to haul it aboard. Thinking they had snagged it on something below the water, they all peered over the edge of the boat to see if they could make out what it had got snagged on. To their astonishment the net was alive with a huge catch, bulging and churning with all kinds of fish. Their fatigue evaporated immediately as the adrenaline surged through their veins. The catch was so big it threatened to capsize the boats. All except Peter and John were transfixed by the catch. These two were looking to the shoreline, to the man whose attention was now focussed on a fire he'd kindled, no longer watching them once they had cast their net. Their hearts pounded and as their eyes met, John said, "It's the Lord!" Peter then did the only rational thing he could think of, which was to get dressed before jumping into the water. Others may have shed their clothing before attempting to swim for shore, but not Peter. He was going to meet his Master and wanted to be dressed to meet him, not stripped as he was for work. The water between them was an obstacle that would never stop him. He arrived on shore before the others, soaked, breathless and shivering from the cold water and the excitement of once again being in the presence of his risen Lord.

The others were not far behind Peter, but arrived a lot drier than he, save for their wet legs as they got out of the boat to land this monumental catch, still thrashing and writhing in the net, which somehow was managing to contain them without splitting.

The fish and the bread which had been cooking over fire while they were still out on the sea was ready to eat when they landed. It was very welcome and the warmth of it brought life back to numbed, sore fingers and filled their hungry bellies. The warmth from the fire started to drive out the early morning chill from their weary bones, although it was going to take a much bigger fire to dry out the soaking wet Peter.

The realisation that it was Jesus on the shore line only hit the other disciples once Peter had gone overboard, by which time they could not let go of the net. The excitement of landing such a miraculous catch was just a precursor to the excitement they all felt once again by being in the presence of Jesus. They all stood on the shore and shook, teeth chattering, partly because of the chill and fatigue and partly from the exhilaration of landing the catch, but mostly from the unparalleled thrill of being with Jesus again. This man, this Son of God, Messiah, the One so longed for throughout the ages, the One prophesied about by the great prophets of old, so full of promise, so endued with power for the miraculous, so holy, so strong yet so gentle, so wronged and yet always so ready to forgive.

You never really knew what was coming next when you were with him: blind men receiving their sight, dead children raised back to life, the multiplication of a boy's lunch, or a fierce confrontation with the religious hierarchy. And this morning... this morning... the risen Lord of Glory cooked breakfast for them, an act in their culture more commonly carried out by their mothers or wives. Never a man. But Jesus was no ordinary man. As each drew near the fire, Jesus handed them a warm, flat loaf of bread with a large piece of steaming hot fish on it.

After they had all eaten their fill and there always seemed to be enough food when Jesus was around, Jesus suggested they take their catch into the town before the flies had the best of it. It hadn't taken long for the flies to be drawn to the catch and they started to buzz and circle excitedly about the fish, like badly behaved children chasing each other round and round. As some of the men started to put the fish into baskets, Jesus took Peter aside and asked him to walk with him a little way from the others. Peter did so, but was self-consciously aware of his clumsy, unusual gait, which he had to adopt as his sodden heavy garments wrapped themselves around his legs, preventing a normal movement as they walked.

Jesus was not oblivious to Peter's discomfort, but He did not let Peter know how strange he looked as he walked this way. Neither did he make any reference to odd squelching noises coming from Peter's sandals as he walked, or to his grimacing as the cold material clung to him as he tried to adjust his heavy garments so he could move more normally. Peter looked ridiculous. Peter felt ridiculous. Peter had consciously taken a step back from their calling, knowing he was not up to the task and had resolved to return to fishing. But Jesus loved Peter too much to let him miss out on what he had called him to. There was nothing that Peter could have done which would have diminished this love that Jesus had for him. It was as if Jesus had specifically chosen the moment that Peter had resolved to resume his lowly life as a fisherman once more, to call him back to that work for which he had been called aside for in the Kingdom of God.

"How was the bread I made for you?" Jesus asked

"Lovely, thank you," Peter replied, a little surprised at the seemingly banal question.

"… and the fish?"

"Umm… again… lovely… thank you… and very welcome," he paused, thought for a moment, then went on. "You didn't have to…" Peter started to tell Jesus he didn't have to go to all that effort of cooking them breakfast, but stopped almost as soon as he'd started. He had so often been ready to tell Jesus that he didn't have to do this or that… didn't have to wash his feet… didn't have to give himself up to the authorities… and so on. None of his protests were meant to insult or correct. They were just wrong, ill-timed, or simply ill-judged, undermining Jesus' purpose in the moment. Maybe for the first time, he had the wisdom to shut up and let Jesus make the point he wanted Peter to understand.

As they walked and squelched slowly along the path that ran parallel to the shore line behind the scrub that separated them from the others, Jesus asked Peter three times if he loved him more than the others. Above anything else in all the world, Peter most earnestly wanted to reassure Jesus that he did and said, "Yes, Lord you know that I love you." Then after he had said this he wanted to go on to add that '…he was so sorry about letting him down, for being a disappointment, for not measuring up and he was especially sorry for denying him on the night he was arrested. But after his initial response that, yes, he did love him, Jesus said something quite unexpected before Peter could start the apology he had been working on and refining whilst eating the bread and fish moments earlier.

"Feed my lambs," he said.

Feed my Lambs? Peter ran the request through his characteristically muddled head. Feed my lambs..? Feed my lambs…? While he was trying to set that statement into their current context, Jesus asked him again if he loved him more than the others, and Peter looked at him quizzically and repeated his earlier response; "Yes Lord, you know that I love you," as if Jesus hadn't heard him. Then, as before, he wanted to go on to add that '…he was so sorry about letting him down… being a disappointment… not measuring up, and he was especially sorry for denying him on the night he was arrested…" He needed to explain that he would never do that again, but again, Jesus cut across his apology. As if he, that is Jesus, had something more important to say. More important than Peter's apology. But what Jesus said was essentially similar to his last request.

"Take care of my sheep," Jesus said to him.

Take care of my sheep…? Peter weighed it against the previous invitation to feed his lambs.

Then Jesus asked him a third time, "Simon Bar Jonah, do you love me?"

Peter was hurt that Jesus had asked him the same question three times. Did Jesus not believe him? Peter replied, "Lord, you know all things. You know that I love you," and Peter knew Jesus knew his heart and the truth of his responses to these questions. Then it started to dawn on him what Jesus was doing each time he cut across his well-rehearsed apologies, like the gradual clearing of the lilac-grey miasma that lay over the water that morning, just blurring the edges of where land met sea.

He looked at Jesus' face; he was neither smiling nor frowning. He searched Jesus' eyes for meaning and found in them the eternity of him searching his own. In them he saw unconditional acceptance of him, love for him and a concern, a deep compassion. In that moment he felt understood by Jesus. It was not that Jesus had not understood him, but at that moment Peter realised Jesus had always understood him perfectly and had always loved him unconditionally.

What Jesus was doing now reminded him of the parable Jesus would tell of the prodigal son who had dishonoured his Father. The son who, after squandering his inheritance on wild living, finally came to his senses and decided to return home with a sincere, but well-prepared apology for the Father he had so publically dishonoured, offering to be accepted as a servant rather than his son. But that father in the parable had been looking out for his errant son, scanning the horizon for any sign he was returning. As soon as the son had decided to return home his Father ran to him, embraced him and would not let his son complete the apology that he had prepared and would not accept him on any terms other than as his beloved son. He reinstates him without caveat or condition because he loved him and was just so glad that he was alive and had returned to him. Peter knew in that parable Jesus was showing his Heavenly Father's willingness to accept returning prodigals, to forgive and reinstate. But… but… was that what Jesus was doing to him now?

Jesus had asked the same question three times, effectively cutting short Peter's own expression of regret each time. Peter earnestly replied with the same affirmation of love and after the third time he did this, Peter felt something dissolve in him, which had held him in torment since that night of Jesus' arrest. The three opportunities Jesus gave Peter to affirm his love for him seemed to put salve on the wounds Peter had inflicted on himself since denying Jesus those three times.

More than this though, Jesus was asking him to feed and look after his sheep; to take care of the flock that was so precious to him. If Jesus wanted him to do this, he would. Not because he felt he had the wherewithal to do it. Quite the contrary in fact. But simply because Jesus had asked him to. Peter's squelching sandals, sodden clothes and awkward gait made Peter look anything but a leader, but that was what he was created to be, because Jesus had ordained it. There was no refinement in Peter, there were no airs or graces about him that would have fit him for service in the temple, or even a local village synagogue for that matter.

There is something about being the only one with the sodden

clothing, squelchy sandals and an awkward gait on a morning when all others about you are neat and tidy that marks you out for leadership in the Lord's eyes. The decision was made long before this morning though. Jesus had told Peter when they'd first met that he would build his church on him, but even before then, his Heavenly Father had created within Peter a heart and mind with the capacity to love and serve his Son. Peter just never actually believed it. He was perfect to shepherd this fledgling church that was so precious to Jesus. The fully clothed leap into the water, while others stayed dry on board the boat, was further proof that Peter was the man for the job, and Jesus blessed that in him. Peter's heart betrayed him beautifully. He could not hide his love for the Lord, and what better quality to be blessed with to lead the church. To show by example how to love the Lord their God with all their heart, soul, mind and strength, and to love their neighbours as themselves.

There would be plenty of rational, sensible, highly qualified, intelligent leaders that would follow Peter over the centuries to come, but too few would carry these qualities which Peter had in abundance, because future leaders would too often be chosen by men, not God. Leaders that would be safe and sensible. Too many "Peters" would be overlooked because of the risks they posed. The man Jesus Himself would probably have been passed by because of the risks he posed, and that sadly would be the fate of the majority of the church once it became established and controlled by men. It was inevitable that Peter was going to make some mistakes, but he loved the Lord and was so eager to please him and to do his will that he would not be beaten by the mistakes, but learn from them and move forward as Jesus would have him do.

To say Jesus continued to appear to the disciples gives the impression of ghostly apparitions spooking them periodically as they went about normal life, reminding them of his death. He in fact met with them in much the same way he had before his death. He sat and ate with them, continued to teach them about His kingdom and the part he had for them to play within it. Peter was strengthened during these times, as were the others and when the time came for them to return to Jerusalem to go up for the feast of Pentecost, they were ready to face the scene of their darkest hour. But this time it was different. It was true that the authorities could not kill Jesus a second time. He had already won that battle once and for all. But what did the trip have in store for this Jesus-less group? It was frequently a topic of conversation, but the truth was nobody knew. While some only saw the clouds in the sky, others only saw the sunlight breaking through the clouds.

SOUTH AGAIN

The journey back to Jerusalem for the festival of Pentecost seemed to take forever. The distances between their preferred stopping-off points seemed to have gotten longer and the road more uneven than last time they travelled it. It hadn't, but it just felt like it had.

When it had become known in and around Capernaum that Peter and the other disciples intended to travel back to Jerusalem for Pentecost, a lot of opinions were shared about whether this was a good idea or not. The overwhelming view was that they were in danger of becoming excessive... overly zealous perhaps... even irresponsible by shirking domestic obligations. Not all those who lived and farmed in the north could afford to take the time out from their labours to travel south for the festivals, so these disciples of Jesus were gossiped about in less than complimentary terms.

"How could they afford to go up to Jerusalem twice this year?"

"Where did they get their money from to do this?"

"How can they leave their parents behind... their land behind... their boats behind... to do this again?

Not all the talking about them was behind their backs. Some of their neighbours felt it their duty to confront them face to face, challenging the wisdom of risking another pilgrimage to Jerusalem "... and so soon after their last trip".

"Look what happened to you last time..." was the common theme, implying the same, or worse would happen if they attempted the journey again. It was said by those that professed to know such things that more bandits were operating in the hills between Galilee and Jerusalem now, waiting for groups of unsuspecting pilgrims to prey on. "Groups of pilgrims like you" was emphasised with a finger pointed at the individual being warned, in case the rather obvious point was missed.

It was true that many in the land had been driven to desperate means to feed themselves and the numbers had increased by the evermore burdensome taxation being levied on them. Many had had to sell their land, or sell their bodies, and it was true: some were even driven to banditry in preference to begging as a means of avoiding inevitable starvation.

In Mosaic Law there was the expectation that every devout male Jew would "present himself before the Lord" three times a year at the Feast of Unleavened Bread, the Feast of Weeks (Pentecost) and the Feast of Booths. However, these passages in scripture were interpreted differently by different groups, so the commandment to "go up" to Jerusalem might be observed once every few years, or perhaps only once in a lifetime. Hence the neighbours' seemingly well-meant counsel for the disciples to exercise moderation rather than what appeared to be over-zealous religious excesses. Some would-be-pilgrims gave weight to these portents of danger and doom and opted to stay behind rather than risk travelling. But notwithstanding the praise and relief expressed by their families for "coming to their senses", there remained a nagging doubt about the decision they'd made. An invisible, relentless and undefinable pull kept their hearts and minds on Jerusalem. As they went about their daily business, as they ate their meals and lay on the beds at night that eventually caused some to impulsively sneak out of their homes before dawn to join the band of travellers congregating on the edge of the village. When everyone was present the group moved off, picking up the road that ran round the edge of the sea, southward towards who knew what…?

The weather at this time of the year was hotter than when they had last made the journey and despite their initial enthusiasm for the trip each disciple seemed to have something that impeded their travelling. New sandals acquired by some for the trip in the belief that old ones wouldn't survive the rigours of the journey quickly started to rub in different places to the ones they replaced. The rubbing quickly produced sores, which required rudimentary bandages to be stuffed between the tough new leather and the tender skin of his feet and ankles. Contrasting with this, other's sandals broke on the journey and had to be temporarily fixed until they could be properly repaired at the next town. Repairs undertaken weren't always strong enough and further repairs were subsequently required at the next town or village they came to, each causing a further delay to their progress. One struggled with headaches, another with back pains. A few suffered from upset stomachs, symptomatic of some poor quality food purchased en route. And so it went on, all the way down from Galilee to Jerusalem.

They seemed to get more easily irritated with each other, but tried not to show it, knowing where all these discouragements were coming from and what their intended purpose was. Even so, the tiredness they felt from travelling made even the most innocuous mannerism irksome after spending days together. The snoring at night, the complaints about the food they shared. The cost of the trip, which was not so well-funded this time, possibly because Jesus was no longer travelling with them. It was this latter detail that was at the root of all their discomfort. This felt like one trip too many. If they were honest with themselves, they would not have felt at liberty to grumble so freely if Jesus was walking with them. Nor would they have felt like this was an unnecessary ministry trip if he was still with them. They would have gladly followed his lead, happy to be with him, ministering as he directed. But they were on their own again now, if a large group can be described as being on its own.

Jesus' words to Peter on that morning by the Sea of Galilee still resonated with him: "Feed my sheep". Look after my flock. So Peter did what he could to ignore trifling irritations that affected him personally and looked out for the weaker ones in the group who may be doing the very best they could, but because of their own personal challenges, be they physical, emotional or matters of faith, found the journey back to Jerusalem particularly tough this time. So Peter walked with these ones, as he'd seen Jesus do when he used to travel with them. There were times when Jesus had said they were going to a certain town or village and they'd set off in that direction. At times when the journey got tough the fitter ones would keep up a pace at the front of the group, but often Jesus would travel with those struggling at the back. Not cheering them on as if they were in a race, but by being a comfort to them, carrying their bundles. Showing them how they were vital to the mission they were on, but never patronising. There were many times when those who had pressed on ahead had to come back and find the group Jesus was walking with, because they'd stopped to minister to someone the front group had walked past in their hurry to get to their destination. Often the miracle would have already occurred by the time they had come back, witnessed by those who could only manage the slower pace, and oh what a tonic it was for them.

So Peter took the loads of the stragglers for a time, cracked a few jokes and did what he could to bring smiles to their faces. He would start a song, usually one of the Psalms they had always sang as they travelled up to the City. His hoarse gravelly voice was most unsuited to singing, but it encouraged others similarly challenged to join in unselfconsciously. He would ask if they remembered occasions when Jesus had done this or said that. These times of sharing personal stories of the things they had seen or benefitted from themselves always brightened the mood of the travelling party. The hours on the road then seemed to pass more quickly.

Because of his quiet serving nature Peter started to stand out among the group of believers as the obvious leader and most were happy to follow his lead, knowing it had been Jesus' will for him to do this. It had been John who, overhearing the conversation between Jesus and Peter, had recounted the gist of it to the others. Not as a gossip, but to confirm Peter's reinstatement as a key disciple. Not that it was necessary, but Peter himself had started to doubt he had any role; anything to contribute to the group and John did what he could to help encourage him in his calling.

The tired straggle of believers trudged and limped along the road that eventually took them through Bethany and past the home of Mary, Martha and Lazarus. These three had been hoping the disciples would come up for the festival and were desperately keen to meet with them again. When they had heard they were approaching Bethany, they ran out to meet them on the road. There were huge embraces and kisses for all and from all the sweaty dusty travellers. This took quite some time because the number of travellers was quite large and the stragglers who found the last few miles particularly tough came in smaller groups of threes and fours, with a red-faced Peter walking with the last group. He was carrying their bundles up the hill, sweating in the heat of the late afternoon's sun, looking more like a beast of burden than a leader.

Lazarus ran to help Peter with the bundles and after a huge hug and kiss on both Peter's sweaty cheeks, Lazarus brought the bundles up the final stretch of road and deposited them in the shadow of a low stone wall by the entrance to his property that faced the centre of the village. Mary and Martha, with a couple of others, ran to the well to draw water for the thirsty crowd who had started to rest their weary feet, finding immediate shade under the assortment of oak, sycamore and pomegranate trees that were dotted about the village. Peter called after them with a weary smile to let them know that he could drink a pitcher full all by himself. To Lazarus, Peter looked happy. Certainly a lot happier than when they had last seen him. Then he looked like he carried the cares of the world upon his shoulders. Today, he looked exhausted, but happy. Quite sweaty, but at peace. Lazarus wanted to know all, but as eager as he was to know what had happened since they had last seen each other, he let his friend rest, cool down, drink and eat before plying him with questions.

Lazarus and his sisters insisted they spent the night with them, but their numbers were too great to accommodate them all under the one roof, so some stayed with their neighbours in the village. The hospitality they received was no different to that when Jesus had been their celebrated companion. Many were delighted to be able to host these dear, honourable friends of Jesus and rather than struggling to find accommodation for them, they had to turn down some willing hosts, promising they would share their table next time they come through.

Martha, famed for her hospitality, provided for these weary travellers magnificently, as she always had. The fine foods and comfortable surroundings were such a tonic to Peter, James, and John. Jesus' mother, brothers and sisters for whom dining with this family from Bethany that they had heard so much about, was something of a new experience, also joined the regular beneficiaries.

The disciples told their hosts about the times they had met with Jesus since their return to Galilee; what he had said to them, even that he'd cooked them breakfast on one occasion. Like everyone they told, the three from Bethany wanted to know every detail. Where…? What…? When…? How often…? After much food and storytelling they became aware that their guests had become really quite tired. While Peter was talking, John would be dozing off, only jolting half-awake when Peter asked him to corroborate something he'd been saying. John's bleary apology brought the evening's discussion to a close, with Lazarus saying to his sisters, "Maybe it would be fairer if we continued this in the morning once our guests have had some proper sleep." John thought this a sound idea and muttered as much, although as he said this he'd already sunk down on to his cushion and was fast asleep before he had even finished his sentence.

The next morning the group's various hosts busied themselves preparing the morning's meal and the pleasant smell of bread baking filled the air in the village. Peter, Lazarus, James and John talked of many things and in particular their accommodation for the feast. They would like to use the upstairs room they had stayed in on their last visit. Ahaz had offered it to them last time they were in the city, but they had not been able to get word to him yet of their intention to avail themselves of his offer and were concerned they might miss the opportunity if they didn't speak to him soon. Lazarus reassured the men that they would always be welcome to stay in Bethany, and the villagers' eagerness to host this band of believers the previous night was testament to the fact. Peter thanked Lazarus, but thought it would be best if they stayed as one group as far as it was possible to do so. The Lord did tend to drop into meet with them from time to time (as bizarre as that sounded to him when he said it out loud) and it would be a shame if they could not all be together on such occasions when He did. Lazarus agreed and said he would go with Peter into the city that morning and discuss the possibility of renting the upper room for a couple of weeks.

It was strange walking down the Mount of Olives once more, heading towards the city, with the Temple towering imposingly above them, seemingly immoveable and eternal. Despite being bone weary from the journey down from Galilee, James and John also went with Peter and Lazarus on this errand. Not because they needed to add weight to any dispute, or numbers to any fight (although that was still a possibility in their minds), but it gave them some purpose and they enjoyed Lazarus's company enormously and walking allowed them to talk freely.

Their short journey from Bethany across the Kidron Valley into the city took them past the garden of Gethsemane, the place where they had often retired to when they were with Jesus because of the peace and solitude it offered the group. Now it held other memories for them, as they tramped flatfooted down the steep road, passing it on their left. Certainly for Peter it was now a place he associated with disappointment and failure, where his hopes and dreams seemed to have abandoned him that night. Like a great ship slowly leaving port without him, driven by the wind in its sails giving it a slow, but determined, unstoppable momentum as he stood and watched helpless to prevent it. Its purpose and mission calling; its momentum greater than his inertia. Peter ran his splayed fingers through his thick, black hair and remembered that night, which seemed so long ago now. As he recalled his actions and state of mind that night, just a few weeks back, he looked at them with a new found maturity, much as an old man recalls the folly of his youth with the regret that only comes with the wisdom accumulated throughout a lifetime. But there was no 'life time' between that night and now. Maybe it was that one encounter with Jesus that chilly morning on the shores of Galilee; that one moment with him, when he was at his lowest point, his most ridiculous looking, his most self-conscious, acutely aware of his failings. That moment more than all the other times, the fun times, the exciting times. That was the moment when he felt his forgiveness. Yes, he thought, that may be the difference in him today, compared to the Peter of a few weeks ago.

As he looked for the tree he'd spent those hours under, in anguish of soul, his eyes caught sight of a small flash of white between the trunks. It was the young goat that had been tethered in the garden that night. Claudia had slipped her tethering today and she skipped with a clank of her bell, over to the low stone wall to see who was passing by; dragging her leash and its inadequate peg behind her. Peter looked at her inquisitive face and smiled as she looked up at him, sniffing the air between them. The others paid her no attention.

Pilgrims arriving in the city, like travellers arriving in any unfamiliar city for that matter, stand apart from the locals in many ways. Despite their best efforts to disguise the fact, lest their naivety attract those who would take advantage of their vulnerability, they stand apart. Residents do not go about their daily business gawping at the views, or the impressive civic buildings. Residents will typically know where they are going. They will not stop at intersections in roads trying to determine whether they should go left, right, or straight on. Nor do they look around trying to determine if they are on the wrong road altogether… and "maybe we should have turned right back there…"? Visitors become aware, or if they are not, they will soon be made aware that their conspicuous and awkward indecision is becoming a problem, holding up those who know where they are going, need to get to where they are going in a hurry, so they can deliver their burden, which is increasing in mass with every passing second they are stuck behind the indecisive tourist. And "never mind the view"!

However, the inescapable grandeur of the temple in Jerusalem was unlike anything else, anywhere in the world and even from a distance its design and position atop Mount Moriah was awe inspiring. As breathtaking as it was from a distance, up close its grandeur simply dwarfed you. In the shadow of its walls you felt a worthless, impoverished wretch, trespassing almost, yet divinely granted the privilege of being allowed to stand in its shade and to let your unworthy eyes cast their uncertain gaze upon such beauty and magnificence. It was utterly breath taking. It possessed a lavish splendour from its vast rectangular foundation stones, weighing several tonnes each, through to its clean, angular architectural symmetry of the numerous courts, the high towers, the magnificent gates and the opulence of the precious metals used throughout. But it was its tangible holiness more than anything else that kept the pilgrim rapt in speechless wonder. The noises from within and the smell of the animals' blood and the smoke from the altar, fire consuming the sacrifices, gave the impression the place was alive, breathing. Residents, privileged to live in close proximity to this holiest of places, understood the effect it had on those not so familiar with living in its shadow, and were perhaps a little more forgiving of visitors bumping into things, into each other and bumping into them as they walked slowly, heads inevitably turned upwards and sideways, looking over their shoulders rather than in the direction they were walking. The building gave the impression of being built *by* God, not by men *for* God. Its permanence and seeming eternality were a palpable reflection of the God it was built to honour. Simply, magnificently awe inspiring. The priests that ministered therein moved theatrically about their tasks with an air of the Almighty God about them. Their power unquestioned, unchallenged, seemingly endorsed by the tethered sheep and goats that meekly yielded to their knives.

Only a flock of Swifts seemed unawed by their surroundings as they swooped and careened in wide arcing formations, silhouetted against the blue sky, screeching disrespectfully at the tops of their voices, before periodically disappearing at speed into crevices in the walls where they nested messily.

When the four men arrived in the city at the house where they had previously boarded, their hearts sank as it looked like another group of pilgrims were occupying the upstairs room they had hoped that they would be able to rent. They knocked on the door and called out the proprietor's name: "Ahaz! Are you home?"

His wife Esther answered the door, with her youngest daughter clinging to her skirts. She looked blankly at the four men, who for a moment looked like all the other pilgrims in the city who had been knocking on her door for the past few days looking for lodgings. She started to explain how they were over-booked and was sorry that she could not offer them lodging on this occasion when she recognised Peter, then John, then, "… Oh… Oh, God be praised!! You've come back!! Oh, please forgive me. Come in dear brothers, come in! Oh thank God you've come back!" Esther seemed deeply moved by their presence.

"Please wait here," she said. "I'll send one of my sons to fetch my husband. He's not far; he's just gone to take some food round to a poor soul a few doors down…" and with that she fetched a young lad from the back of the room and told him to tell his father the friends of the Teacher were here to see him. The boy eyed the four men momentarily then shot off down the street as fast as his sandals would carry him. He returned a few moments later with a concerned looking father, who, on seeing the four men, offered his profoundest apologies for not being at home when they arrived, enveloping each of them in his enormous embrace. The men waved away his apologies as completely unnecessary, but the man still looked concerned.

He said, "I presume you are after the room upstairs…?"

"If it is available, yes we would like to rent it," said Peter, "but it looks like you have guests already," pointing in the direction of the rafters. He had become aware of movement in the room above them.

"Oh, no don't worry about them," the man went on. "They know it is a temporary arrangement until you arrive… if you were to arrive. I'm sorry, I really didn't know if I would see any of you again."

"Please don't apologise," said Peter. "I should have sent word to you. It was foolish for us to set off without making prior arrangements."

Ahaz said, "We did have an arrangement that you would come back and use the room, if it was in God's will…" and shooting his arms up in the air in celebration he said "… and it seems it is! God is great!"

"Thank you for you generous hospitality, but we cannot evict your current guests. I will not… we will not, be responsible for them being without lodgings during this festival. None of this is their fault. We can stay at Bethany…"

"Leave it to me," said Ahaz, as he backed out of the door and skipped round the corner of the house and ran up the steps, taking them two at a time, to speak with the group upstairs.

Peter's plea not to do this followed him out of the door, but missed its target, disappearing in the small cloud of dust kicked up by Ahaz as he ran his familiar route upstairs. He can move quickly for a big man, thought Peter.

The upstairs door was open and the men could hear greetings exchanged, then a long explanation, followed by a series of questions about the men downstairs and then some further instructions and directions from Ahaz. Shortly after this there were three pairs of footsteps coming down the steps and Ahaz reappeared in the doorway, followed by a couple of the men, presumably from the party upstairs. Ahaz called for his son and told him to go with these men to the boy's uncle's house and to ask him to offer these men lodgings for the festival, as his friends from the north had arrived as expected.

Once the boy and the two lodgers had left, the now slightly perspiring owner turned with a satisfied smile to the four men, who had watched all this going on in silence, and said, "There! All taken care of. I had already asked my brother to be prepared to take in guests at short notice in case you turned up. The family group upstairs knew I had promised the room to you if you were free to come to the festival this year."

"How can I thank you?" Peter asked. The owner waved away the suggestion in the same way the men had waved away his apology earlier.

Peter then said, "Previously there were those in our group who looked after the money and attended to such matters such as paying for rent for accommodation like this." Peter was referring to Judas Iscariot in particular, who he believed had previously paid for the room in advance of their lodging last time. He believed this because when it was time for the party to leave last time he asked what they owed the man and he had said, "Nothing at all. It was all covered. Thank you."

"I am sorry," Peter went on, "but I have no idea what the agreed rent is for your room." The man again waved his hand in the air and smiled. "There is no cost for you or your friends. It is an honour to have you under my roof. You are family for as long as you wish to stay here. You always have been and always will be."

"I cannot thank you enough, Sir," Peter said. "You are too generous." He had fully expected to pay for lodgings at one of the busiest times of year for the city. He and Lazarus had discussed this on the walk into the city and Lazarus had offered to cover the cost if the groups' funds were unduly stretched by it.

They said they would await the return of the men, who had gone to find his brother to make sure they were not causing them any difficulties and within half an hour the two men had returned and were excited about their new accommodation and couldn't wait to tell their families. Their new lodgings were closer to the temple and from the roof top they could see into the courts. Well, they could see the entrance to the outer courts, at least, and all the comings and goings thereof. It even had its own well!

Peter thanked the owner once more for his generosity and made a point of going upstairs to apologise to the families there for the inconvenience they were putting them through, but they were already hurriedly packing their belongings together, excited about the prominence of their new lodgings and paid little attention to Peter.

Back downstairs Peter said they would return later that day, giving everyone enough time to sort out their new arrangements, but as he was speaking the families had already started to decamp from the upper room and were running past Peter and the owner with badly tied bundles of bedding in their arms, eager to lay claim to their new, temporary dwellings before anyone else did.

The five men stopped their conversation for a moment and watched with some amusement as the men, women and children from the upstairs room fell over each other in their haste as they ran past, dropping the occasional item they were carrying in their rush to get to the new lodgings.

"Sure, my brother has a nice house," the owner said with some resignation to the four men, then raising his voice to address his departing tenants. "But is mine such a flea-infested hovel that you must run from it like you're running from the plague?" he shouted after the families as they scurried down the street, more for dramatic effect than out of any real sense of anger. He was actually glad that he was now free to host his friends from Galilee once more.

He turned back to Peter, James and John and hunching his shoulders with a wry smile, he said, "It looks like the place is yours already... If you still want it ... after those ingrates..." the last words he shouted back down the street, again in the direction of the last of the fleeing families. Then, softening his tone as he turned back to his friends, he said, "It will be cleaned and readied for you before you return."

"Thank you again," the four men said as they were about to leave.

"Tonight you will share my table," Ahaz said.

Peter thanked him, but explained there were quite a few of them. The man enquired just how many "quite a few" was. When Peter told him, he raised his eyebrows and said that is perfectly fine, but we may have to use meat as the garnish to the meal, rather than the meal itself, and he laughed at his own joke. "Seriously, you will join me and my family tonight. We loved the Teacher and our hearts have been broken ever since last Passover when they took him and… and did what they did…" Ahaz had to stop as his voice began to crack with emotion and he drew imaginary, circular objects in the air with shaky fingers to describe what his words failed to. Neither Peter, John nor Lazarus knew what the gestures were meant to convey, but this man's good heart did, and that's all that mattered. Ahaz looked down at his feet for a moment, then up again at Peter. "We have heard so many fanciful rumours since his passing and since you left us that we do not know what to believe. Please eat with us and tell us everything so that we may know the real truth."

"We will be glad to," Peter said and the others joined in with their thanks and promises to do just as he'd asked.

As they walked back to Bethany James said to no one in particular, "I'm sure Judas said he had to pay handsomely for that room…" the others thought the same, but said nothing.

Back in Bethany aching limbs were put to work once more, bundling up bedding and belongings for the final leg of their journey into the city. But rather than carrying them, the heaviest bundles were loaded on to Lazarus's donkey to take the last couple of miles into the city.

There were mixed feelings as the group entered the city again. The scene of such horror the last time they were there, followed immediately by fear of further arrests and reprisals. The scattering of the group, the betrayal by and loss of Judas Iscariot, then the unsurpassed glory and wonder of seeing Jesus alive again in their midst. Fear did tug at them. The paranoia of being identified as Jesus' followers made them walk into the city in silence with their heads bowed. What if the authorities, Roman or Jewish, regretted missing their opportunity last time to finally kill off the remainder of Jesus's followers with him and decided to complete the job this time around?

They all seemed to breathe a communal sigh of relief once they were all back in the upper room, with the ill-fitting door wedged shut behind them. But it was only a couple of minutes before they had to open it again because the heat was insufferable at this time of year with it shut. That resolved that little issue then. They would have to be brave enough to leave it open to allow the meagre breeze to circulate the room.

By evening they were all famished. The meats which Ahaz had been roasting all afternoon were receiving their finishing touches and the smells of cooking, which had been wafting in through the windows and doorway all afternoon, were now being further enhanced by the heady aromas of the herb dressings being applied to the hot, golden meats. The smoke from the fragrant oils suffused with rosemary, thyme and mint being driven up towards his guests as they dripped from the succulent meat on to the hot coals of the fires they were being roasted over. The visitors were becoming ravenous and ready to appreciate this feast being laid on for them by their hosts. Ahaz was famed for being as generous of heart and purse as he was himself generously proportioned. This was how they always found him to be.

The evening meal was a proper reunion of good friends. There was a newfound joy in each other's company. Friendships which had been strengthened through adversity and forced separation. Accounts were given of the many and varied appearances of Jesus. Where they had met with him, who was there. (even one time when around five hundred were present!) Ahaz, his family and their friends all listened with undivided attention. Awestruck by these wonderful accounts, "who has ever heard of such a thing?" was said more than once by each of them.

As the night's feasting drew to a close the guests thanked their hosts for their wonderful hospitality and the hosts thanked their guests for all that they had shared with them. The guests, now tired, started to make their way back upstairs to sleep, but the hosts themselves were far from sleep and continued talking over everything they had just been told. "… the risen Jesus had even visited their own house… he appeared to… how many did they say? More than five hundred people at one time! He cooks for them and eats with them!" Over and over their conversations went on through the night.

"…who could sleep after hearing such things? What does it all mean?"

The preparation for the feast of Pentecost carried on in the city with the same momentum it always did, but for the disciples much of it was secondary to the real reason they were there. Jesus had asked them to be present and he met with them again there. Someone said they'd be happy to travel to Rome itself if Jesus asked them to, just so long as they could spend time with him there. They all agreed. However, shortly after this, when Jesus told them they would be his witnesses in Samaria (among other places on Earth) there was a certain amount of shuffling of feet and hoping that that particular instruction was for someone else in the group. It happened while they were eating with him again, this time out on the Mount of Olives some six weeks after the weekend of his resurrection. He'd told them not to leave Jerusalem until they had received the gift His Father had promised them. Jesus went on to talk about a baptism of the Holy Spirit, a baptism of power. This caused some in the group to ask whether this would be the start of the restoration of Israel, an agenda they'd never let go of, holding on to the populist concept of the warrior Messiah and always trying to fit Jesus' words to that specific agenda. The thought of receiving power was a nice one; actually an absolute basic essential, but to witness in Samaria? To witness in Jerusalem would be dangerous enough, as would other parts of Judea. But Samaria? They hated Jews there. And where were the ends of the earth? It sounded like a long way away. Had they heard of Messiah there? Had they heard of Judea there?

Then, it seemed, all too soon the time for further questions was over. Just like that. They had walked outside for no more than a few minutes after what turned out to be their final meal with Jesus. Martha and Mary had provided another pleasant midday meal of lentils, vegetables, pickled fish and fresh bread. They had all eaten well and comforted by the food and the good company had got up to stretch their legs after the meal, as was their custom. Throughout the meal Jesus had been talking about returning to the Father and the disciples being his witnesses. They had not been outside very long when Jesus paused. He turned to look at them and said a few things about loving one another and waiting in Jerusalem, as if they were his closing remarks, then the cloud came. It enveloped them all. In the heat of the midday sun a cloud seemed to descend from nowhere like an autumn fog, but without the damp chill. In fact there was nothing in it so unpleasant as damp, or chill, or darkness about this cloud. Quite the opposite. There was a brightness within the cloud and a comforting embrace within it, like this was somewhere you belonged, a kind of peace, yet a sense of something awesome and terrifying within it too. This was not a natural phenomenon. Jesus was in the midst of it, in fact the very focus of it, it seemed to Peter. It instantly reminded him of that time he had seen this before on Mount Tabor with James and John. They remembered well the sense of awe and terror the cloud had brought that evening. You never got used to it. You could never get accustomed to the awe and the wonder of the nearness of God, for that was what this was. Along with the reverence that was stirred within you, you were also conscious of your own feeble mortality. Your petty mindedness and sinfulness. It was this juxtaposition of the two states that made them start to shake. They all shook as if shivering from a chill brought by the fog, but they were not cold. Far from it. They each prayed silently in the presence of their God, loving him and being loved by him. There was no voice from the cloud today as there had been on Tabor, but the sense of God's holiness was there again.

As the cloud thickened, so did the brightness within it. The brightness grew in their midst. Initially it seemed to come from above them, moving about them, living. It shone from behind Jesus, growing in intensity such that the edges of his features became indistinct. Then, before he was completely obscured from their sight, Peter saw Jesus smile, stretch out his arms as if to embrace one he alone could see. Jesus took a step, then the brilliance of the cloud utterly enveloped him, obscuring him from their view. Then almost as quickly as it came the cloud started to lift and departed from them.

For the final time Jesus was hidden from their sight, though none knew this was the final time. Jesus had already risen from the dead, so there were no longer any absolute finalities. But this was a final supernatural act, one most had not imagined they'd ever see.

As the darling of heaven was once more received back into the glorious presence of his Father, taking his seat beside him in the throne room of heaven, clothed in unimaginable splendour, the small bunch of somewhat bemused and ragtag disciples stood in the swirling dust atop the Mount of Olives clothed in their grubby, crudely woven garments staring at the sky. Each with a question on their lips that had previously been so important they wished they'd had the opportunity to ask just a moment before, but now they seemed utterly inappropriate and meaningless.

As the cloud cleared they continued to stand there, staring into the sky, now squinting and shielding their eyes from the sun. Peter became aware of two men standing just in front of him also, looking up into the sky. He didn't remember seeing these men before. They were dressed quite differently and they certainly weren't part of their group, but they stood in their midst as if they were. They craned their necks, looking up, shielding their eyes from the sun, just as the rest of the group were.

Then, without turning to Peter, the nearest man asked, "Why are you looking into the sky?"

Peter thought these men were trying to see Jesus, just as they had been, but the cloud that had moments before enveloped them had now dissipated and it was obvious there was nothing above them but the brilliant blue of the Judean sky. The two men's continued staring up into the clear expanse of blue seemed to emphasise the pointlessness of standing there any longer. Jesus had gone.

The stranger's comment seemed to bring them to their senses and they wondered how long they had been standing there like that. Suddenly self-conscious, as if caught in a day dream, they dusted themselves off, bent down to pick up staffs and bags where they had been dropped, and readied themselves for their short journey back into the city.

The two strangers spoke again. Neither were looking into the sky anymore. No one was.

"This same Jesus…" said the stranger who'd previously spoken

"Same Jesus," echoed his companion. Peter gave him a furtive glance.

"…who has been taken from you into heaven…" continued the first man "…will come back in the same way you have seen him go into heaven."

"The same way," echoed his companion. Peter gave him another furtive glance.

That was all they said. The strangers and the group stood in silence, looking at each other, weighing the message the strangers had given them. The strangers letting the message be weighed.

"Thank you," said Peter, feeling some response was necessary.

The group, now readied with staffs and bags, started their descent back down the hill towards the city. The two strangers stayed at the top of the hill and watched the confused, lonely and insignificant band of believers trudge away in silence, wondering if they would ever see Jesus again. Once the group were out of sight the two strangers turned, smiled at each other and left.

THE SHAKING

"Here it is Saba!," the little girl called out triumphantly to her grandfather as she entered the house with the lamp, still chewing one of the dates the nice lady next door had given her. She had asked the lady to light the lamp that she had inexpertly filled with oil and trimmed at her grandfather's request. The four year-old had overfilled it and did not know what to do with the wick, so the friendly old lady next door helped her and placed the lit lamp in a dish so she wouldn't burn herself when carrying it back home. She had also placed a couple of fat juicy dates in the dish as a treat for the dear little thing.

"Put it on the table," came the curt response from the storeroom to her left.

Carefully carrying the lit oil lamp, she lifted the dish it now sat in, on to the corner of the table and took the last date from the dish.

Her grandfather had to send her out to ask one of the neighbours to light the lamp because the fire in the brazier had been allowed to go out. As the sun had now slipped down below the city's skyline a deep gloom settled in the room they shared; a gloom which matched his mood. The lamp brought an uncertain light to the big room, but did nothing to improve the old man's sulk, which was a bitter resentment for being left to fend for himself for the past couple of hours.

Lois sat on her favourite cushion and stared into the flame as she chewed her last date. When she looked up to see what her grandfather was doing the room seemed darker than it did a moment ago because of the coloured spots that now danced in front of her eyes. She blinked to try and clear her vision then looked up at the rafters, which had just creaked again. This caused a small cloud of dust to be released that sparkled when it reached the lamp's flame. There were a lot of people upstairs tonight. She'd seen and heard their arrivals throughout the day and the number of visitors had increased significantly with the arrival of the friends of her parents from Galilee over the past few days. Her parents were up there with them now, as were her older siblings and half of Jerusalem, it seemed.

She could hear Saba grumping about in the storeroom, so she placed the date pit on the table and slid off her cushion to see what he was doing. She could tell he wasn't happy. He was evidently hungry and his meal wasn't ready. Mother would normally have made sure everything was ready for him when he wanted it, but today – well, in fact for the past few days, she had seemed preoccupied with the growing number of guests in the room upstairs.

In the dark storeroom she could make out the figure of Saba. It looked like he had been dipping his hands into all the various storage jars, which were now uncharacteristically open with their lids missing. She could tell he had been sampling their contents because his fingers were still glistening with oil. This was something she knew her mother would not approve of. Saba was foraging alternately between jars of dates and jars of olives, popping the fruit into his mouth with his left hand and spitting the stones into his right hand once he'd chewed most of the flesh from the fruit. The stones were then placed on the ledges around the room to be found by his daughter in law later, once she'd deigned to come back downstairs to look after him as she was supposed to be doing now.

The old man bent down and sniffed a soot-stained terracotta cooking pot in the corner of the room. He could not see the contents in the poor light, but it smelled like food and it felt half full. He groaned as he lifted the pot, straightening up as far as his curved spine would allow him. Carrying the pot in both hands, he shuffled back into the main room of the house, heading for the small beacon of the lamp, which was positioned precariously close to the edge of the table. The pot was rested on the edge of the table next to the lamp, which he lifted to help him examine the contents of the pot.

"Lentils," he said to Lois as much as to himself.

They had had this stew a couple of nights ago and although the lamplight showed a light, downy fuzz of mould had since grown on the cold stew, his old eyes couldn't detect it. He returned the lamp to a more central position on the table and placed the pot alongside it next to some flat breads that Lois's mother had baked that morning and had left on the table for the family. The bread was now dry and hard, but still edible. The old man returned to the store room to find some dishes. There was a small pile of them, from which he chose two that had only the lightest remnants of previous meals still on them. Lois watched him return and he dipped the first small dish into the pot, scooping out a solidified lump of the cold stew and set it before the little girl. She smiled and politely said, "Thank you, Saba." Lois looked suspicious at the furry grey lump that sat in the dish before her, looking as much like a small animal as it did a lentil stew. Saba lifted the second dish to repeat the action for himself, then set it down again, opting instead to eat directly from the pot using pieces of the hard bread to scoop the cold stew into his mouth. He took one large, round loaf from the stack and handed it to Lois, who mouthed a silent "Thank you", with an uncertain smile as she took it. Holding the loaf in her two small hands, it practically obscured her tiny frame. He then took the next loaf for himself and started to break the bread and feed himself hungrily.

The noise in the room above them started to increase again. The guests had been fairly quiet, considering how many were up there. Just the constant creaking from the rafters giving away their presence. Lois longed to go up the steps again to see what they were doing, but felt she should stay with Saba to make sure he was okay. She couldn't leave Saba all alone. Her grandfather in turn chose to ignore the noises, preferring instead to suck the soured stew from the dried bread. Lois sat opposite him, crunching on the edge of her loaf that was easily twice the size of her face, fidgeting and wiggling her dirty feet; preferring not to risk the stew. She wouldn't normally be allowed a whole loaf to herself and she enjoyed the novelty of it now. Her eyes never left Saba's face, fascinated by the movement of all his wrinkles and how they worked together to consume the food he was devouring enthusiastically.

Singing started in the room above them. It was simple at first, the hoarse rasping voice of a solitary Galilean taking the lead, soon joined by others picking up his melody. It sounded... special, Lois thought. Important even. She would have thought it holy if the concept had been familiar to her and she tried to hum along to it, but the crunch of the bread made that difficult and she didn't want to annoy Saba, who she knew was trying to ignore it.

Suddenly there was a loud thud as though something, or someone, landed heavily on the floor above them and a light shower of dirt and bits of dead insects rained down from the floor boards above, onto the two diners below. Saba didn't allow it to distract him and he continued to scoop the contents from the pot in front of him, uninterrupted. Lois flicked away some particles that had landed on her bread, before resuming the task of chewing along the edge of the large loaf, looking much like an insect eating a leaf.

When the old man had had his fill he leaned back, belched acceptably and looked across the room to his favourite corner, where he thought he would settle himself before attempting to sleep off the meal. He thought he might be able to sleep if their guests would just stop their nonsense for a moment and behave more respectfully, as was befitting guests in his son's house. As he got up Lois laid down the crescent of her uneaten bread on the table and went to the water jar to get herself a drink.

"Would you like a drink, Saba?" her soft, sweet voice reminding him of her presence in the room, which had for a time been obscured by the loaf.

"No thank you, my dear," his mood mellowing slightly now that he had eaten. He declined the drink more out of concern for the interruption a drink at this late hour would have on his sleep than for any lack of thirst.

Once she'd drunk her fill from the dipping cup, Lois replaced it on its hook, crossed the room and curled up on a cushion near her Saba. She watched him as he settled down and closed his eyes. She listened to the soft melodies emanating from upstairs and the comfort that the songs seemed to carry to her. Very soon, like a lullaby, they caused her to drift off to sleep.

Sometime later, suddenly aware that it had become dark, her mother Esther came down to check on her daughter and father in law. She took a taper from the ledge on the wall and lit two more lamps from the one burning in the middle of the table. A quick scan of the room told her everything she needed to know. The cooking pot and dishes left out, broken pieces of bread strewn over the table and across the floor in the direction of her snoring father in law and the tiny curled frame of her daughter who slept silently close by him.

The furry grey lump sitting in one of the bowls on the table concerned her though.

"Oh, you didn't eat that…" she sighed to herself and looked across at the old man who didn't stir.

Clearing the mess he'd left could be left until the morning, she thought to herself. Esther was keen to get back upstairs as quickly as possible. Tonight's meeting felt distinctly different to all the previous nights and she did not want to be absent from it for a moment longer than absolutely necessary. Thinking three lamps was extravagant, she extinguished one, bent down and scooped up her daughter, who sleepily looped her arms around her mother's neck and buried her face into her shoulder. Esther took one last look at the old man, knowing he could join them upstairs if he changed his stubborn heart, but also knowing he wouldn't. She closed the door behind her as she went outside, turned left along the front of the house and climbed the stairs to the upper room, carrying her daughter in her arms.

As they entered the upper room no one noticed their arrival, apart from those closest to the door, who stepped aside with a knowing smile to let mother and daughter in. The room was packed with around a hundred and twenty people wedged in to it. It was hot from all the lamps that were burning around the walls and from the bodies that rocked back and forth, lost in worship, sweating as they did so in the cramped and stuffy conditions. The singing and praying continued and the heavy presence of God in their midst was so thick and tangible Lois felt she could have reached out her hand and touched Him. Now properly awake, she straightened her body in her mother's arms, signalling that she wanted to be put down, which Esther was glad to do. Once free of her tiny burden Esther crossed her hands over her heart as it swelled again with love for her God. She closed her eyes and once more joined in with the worship, her aching hunger for her God soothed in the simplicity of the melodies and fed by the shared passion for Him. Lois silently wove her way between the adults to find her big sister that she had seen from the height of her mother's shoulder.

* * *

There is nothing quite like the feeling of utter impotence in the face of an impossible commission to drive you to prayer, and so it had started for the group of believers. They had started to gather in the upper room of the house of Ahaz and Esther to pray and to worship, initially because of the impossibility of the commission they had been given, but very soon they did not want to be anywhere else as the sense of expectation grew whenever they met together. As their expectation grew, so did their numbers. It felt like the right thing to do and there was an ease about it and the sense that Jesus was with them as they met like this, despite Him not being physically in the room with them. The room started to get packed out with other believers in the city who joined them. Some had travelled down from Galilee with them, others were residents in and around Jerusalem, those whose lives had already been touched by Jesus at some point and loved him. These were not mournful prayer meetings, but times full of worship songs, intermingled with prayer; punctuated with periods of fellowship and eating together. As the sense of expectation grew no one wanted to leave the meetings, to run errands, prepare food, or to attend to other essentials of life. Once each chore had been completed, the parties quickly and gladly returned to what was becoming an extraordinary and somewhat extended prayer meeting.

When the main feast day of Pentecost came, these prayer meetings had already been running for some days and it was then that the gift Jesus had spoken of, the outpouring and empowering of the Holy Spirit was given to the disciples as they met in that room.

The prayer meetings had started to run on through the night. Those who could stay awake were just caught up in worship and adoration of their Lord, but they were human and each would inevitably succumb to the need for sleep or food. It was in the early hours of the morning on the day of the Feast of Weeks, Shavuot, also known as Pentecost. The time of worship and praying together had been particularly sweet and a quiet had descended upon the room, as it had from time to time on previous occasions. However, on this occasion the quiet lasted longer than previously as each member of the group communed quietly and deeply with their Lord. Some stood, some knelt, some lay prostrate. Peter was worshipping at the far end of the room when he started, ever so slightly, to tremble. This was an unusual sensation, but not unlike the time they stood in the cloud when Jesus was taken up from them. It was a trembling you might associate with fear, or nervous excitement, but there was no fear or nervousness. Rather there was the beginning of a bubbling up of excitement within his chest, almost imperceptible at first, but then it grew in intensity and started to spread down his arms, through his abdomen and into his legs. The shaking started to increase and at first he felt a little self-conscious and popped open one eye to peek at the men next to him. John, Andrew and James all seemed to be caught up in worship, but were each similarly affected with this trembling. Peter could not keep his eye open any longer and had a solitary thought pass through his mind. "I hope this is You, Lord".

As soon as the question was thought, he felt like he had been hit by a big wave. Not the sort that crashed on the shores of Galilee when a storm stirred the waters up, but more like one of the big breakers that rolled in off the Great Sea, near Carmel or at the Port of Caesarea, where the water level would drop from chest deep to below waste deep as the waves grew, before crashing over your head, swamping you, driving you towards the shore. This wave rocked Peter and the shaking intensified. Every part of him was now shaking, apart from his left leg, which he noted and thought curious. This was the only part of his body which seemed to be functioning normally now, and the only thing holding him upright. Then another wave hit him and another and he really needed to steady himself now lest he fall flat on his back taking others with him and possibly causing injuries among those of a slighter build standing near him, or worse among some of the much older and frailer members of the group who he believed were within his immediate fall radius.

Peter, with all his concentrated effort, popped open an eye again to see where John was (believing he was to his immediate right) to see if he could hold on to him for support. To his astonishment John was also shaking with what appeared to be the same intensity as Peter. Every part of John, with the exception of one of his legs (which Peter again thought curious), was also being shaken. John had the expression of one utterly lost in wonder and adoration, almost oblivious to the fact that he was shaking like a leaf on a tree. With some concentration, Peter carefully turned his head to his left, not wanting to lose his balance, like a man standing on one leg on a high wire. His brother Andrew was to his immediate left and Peter was hoping he'd be able to hold on to him to stop himself from falling, but Andrew looked to be in a worse state than Peter was as he was rocking back and forth as well as visibly shaking, seemingly defying gravity. If Peter had attempted to hold on to Andrew he was certain the pair of them would fall and the combined mass of the Bar Jonah brothers landing on one of the more frail members of their group would have inflicted serious crush injuries. At least that was Peter's primary concern, rightly or wrongly. As these thoughts went through Peter's mind another wave of the Spirit hit him and he was concerned and distracted no longer. He just soaked up the glory of the wonderful presence of the Holy Spirit, which had started to be poured out upon them. As a dry sponge swells as it soaks up water poured out upon it, so Peter and all the others in the room soaked up the Holy Spirit as He was poured out upon them, being filled to capacity, then filled again, and again.

All sense of time was lost as wave upon wave of glory crashed in upon the disciples. Some of them were already prostrate under the weight of glory and more and more of them fell with each crashing wave as their flesh gave into the onrushing tide, hopelessly powerless to withstand or control its divine empowering. After some time it felt like the room in which they were meeting was being shaken. Not just the flesh within it, but the actual stone and timber of its construction. A noise accompanied this shaking like a powerful wind, ripping through the fabric of the building. Doors and shutters were blown open and as Peter once more, with all the strength he could muster, forced one of his eyes open. He could see what looked like a fire spreading around the room. Each member of the group looked like a coal in a brazier, burning with an unearthly, heavenly flame. Shutting his eyes, Peter eventually glided to the floor like a leaf falling from a tree, without injuring a soul. The waves had crashed against his defences and overcome them. The rising tide swept all before it. There on the floor the earthquake started in his soul and in the souls of the other believers in the room.

The tectonic plates colliding, which caused this earthquake, were those belonging to the kingdom of Heaven and the kingdom of Earth. One profane, the other holy. One offering grace, mercy and forgiveness, the other built by self and for itself, offering nothing but cold religion. One full of beauty and life, the other ugly and dying. To come into the presence of the Holy, Holy, Holy God is a magnificent and terrifying thing. Only one kingdom will prevail. The other will always have to yield, unable to stand in the presence of the Almighty Creator God, who had just entered that room by His Spirit. Nonsensical thoughts were swept aside, replaced by earnest repentance. Good, godly men knew they were wretched sinners in the pure light of his holy presence. The sins they were happy to tolerate in their lives, hidden in their hearts, unseen by anyone, save the Holy God who now swept the room. They knew they were hell bound, but for the saving grace of God through the blood poured out by His son Jesus the Messiah at Golgotha just a few weeks ago.

As with all earthquakes, it seems it is often the poorly built manmade structures that suffer the most extensive damage, crumbling to rubble within seconds of the first tremors hitting them. The tragedy is that it is these structures that often take the lives they were intended to protect. The earthquake Peter and the other believers in that room were experiencing in their souls had started with the first tremors as the Holy Spirit started to fall upon them and continued with an increasing intensity as aftershock upon aftershock hit them.

Each tremor started to bring down the man-made structures that had been built in their souls over their lifetimes; built to protect themselves, to promote themselves, to preserve their lives. The first buildings to fall were those of fear and doubt as waves of love and forgiveness crashed over them. As these structures fell, other structures around them became weakened as they depended upon them for strength, structures of unhealthy ambition, structures to develop social standing within the group and with society at large. The structure built for the love of money and the security that gave them, soon followed these and crashed into the worthless pile of rubble, now lying where the buildings had once stood. As gaps appeared between buildings others fell more quickly as the powerful, irresistible wind ripped through them, each building collapsing into the rubble of the worthless, fruitless life so carefully constructed and previously held so dear. The landscapes of their souls changed utterly, unrecognisable from that which previously existed there. But far from being barren, it had been made level and fertile, ready for the structures God was now rapidly building within them.

Time stopped, or maybe it passed quickly. You couldn't tell. Peter felt very different as he lay there on the floor. No one spoke for a time. Then a voice in the opposite end of the room said something unintelligible. A brief sentence which sounded like praise, but Peter didn't understand what had been said. The person repeated the phrase and again. Peter thought it sounded like praise, but didn't grasp what had been said. Was it one of the believers who had joined them from one of the neighbouring countries and rather than using local Aramaic to praise God, which was customary in their group, they had used their native tongue? Peter didn't think so, but lay there in silence, dazed. Another voice, this time from close by, said a sentence that again sounded like praise, but was again unintelligible. From the sound of the voice Peter was pretty sure it had come from James, but he was sure that neither James nor his brother John could speak other languages. The next voice came from Peter's "pillow". He hadn't appreciated until just then that when he slid to the floor he'd been lying with his head on his brother Andrew's stomach. That voice came from Andrew and he knew he could barely master his mother tongue of Aramaic, let alone any other. This surprised him and he was about to get up to look at his brother when, like a huge bubble coming up from the depths of Galilee, he burst forth in praise of God in a language he had not previously spoken. He knew exactly the meaning of what he was saying, but it didn't come out in his own tongue. He was shocked and laughed a little because of the surprise of it. All around the room, one after another, different voices started to express their love of God in different languages. It was like fat rain drops just starting to fall randomly, with increasing rapidity, building and building in frequency as just before a heavy downpour. One by one the rain drops plopped into the dry arid dust of their lives. One here, one there. Then another and another, then the staccato, disconnected droplets started to become a shower, the shower became like rainfall and the rainfall became a deluge. And that was how it started. Individual voices expressing their love for the Lord; one after the other they started to come together in a beautiful cacophony of worship as the deluge swept the room, driven by the Spirit of God, enabling the broken flesh in the room to offer forth an acceptable, selfless, holy offering of worship to the Lord.

As the rain fell on that thirsty group the noise grew and grew, and Peter could tell from the voices that it wasn't just the men in his immediate vicinity. As he strained to lift his head from the pillow of his brother's stomach and look across the room, he could see it was the old as well as the young, men and women who were making all the noise. He plopped his head back down on Andrew's stomach and Andrew let out an "Oooff…" as the unexpected weight of his brother's head hit him again. Peter apologised, then said something like "Shamanamanan…" afterwards and smiled to himself.

Andrew responded with, "That's okay brother…" and continued with something that sounded like "Banani-manani-manam… manam…" Peter then felt his pillow jerk and tense as his brother tried to stifle a laugh because he thought it inappropriate. This made Peter smile and Andrew sensed it and with all his might managed to restrict his belly laugh to a much muted "Herrr… herrr…" barely audible to anyone but those in his immediate patch of floor. But there was enough dry tinder in that room to be caught by that one spark of Andrew's muted laugh. Peter snorted and Andrew, who could contain it no longer, let out a huge roar of a belly laugh. As his stomach muscles contracted with the laugh and as he brought his knees up to his chest, Peter's head was catapulted forwards and he rolled on to his side laughing, looking at his brother who had lost all hope of being able to contain his laughter, his face reddening with the exertion of the roar. Those next to them caught the laughter and were immediately undone as they all started roaring with laughter. This shot around the room as more and more of the believers were unable to contain their laughter as a joy like they'd never experienced before burst out of them. This laughter continued and continued and after a while it started to hurt. Really hurt, in the nicest possible way. You wanted to stop because your sides ached, your stomach ached, your back ached. Even your face and jaw muscles ached, but the laughter kept bubbling up. Each time it started to subside, you would see someone in the room who you had never seen laugh that hard, just roaring and roaring with laughter and it would start up all over again. It seemed particularly the case if it was one of the older men or women who would normally be the more serious, restrained and thoughtful members of the group, who were laughing uncontrollably. If eye contact was made all control was lost.

After a time it started to subside and it looked like normal people were occupying the room once more. Then Peter caught sight of Nathaniel, bent over, leaning against the wall holding his side, trying to catch his breath and in some pain saying, "Ooh… ooh… ooh dear…" and panting whilst showing his teeth in some grimace, like he had just sprinted up a steep hill,. That started Peter off again; laughing at Nathaniel's obvious discomfort because he had been laughing too hard for too long. This laughter just rippled around the room again and all the "normal people", who it seemed had momentarily reoccupied the room, were suddenly replaced by those who did not have a sober, sensible bone in their bodies. This went on for some time until all were completely exhausted.

The Spirit continued His ministrations as He touched individuals in different ways. Some continued to worship in languages they'd not learnt. A few seemed like they would never stop laughing and others wept. Actually each in the room seemed to manifest the various different characteristics at different times. Some wept while others laughed. Some stood as still and as silent as stone pillars with hearts and faces turned towards heaven, while others right next to them bounced up and down, up and down with their hands in the air, sweating under the physical exertion, but obviously at peace. And so God continued His beautiful transforming work in the disciples. A work, which to the dispassionate observer may have seemed like chaotic nonsense, but because it was a work of the hands of the Almighty God, it would prove to be world changing. Pivotal. History making.

The residential properties that formed the city of Jerusalem were tightly packed with narrow alley ways between them. The usual dawn chorus of song birds, cockerels and donkeys braying that greeted the city's inhabitants was supplemented that morning by the activities going on in the upper room of the house of Ahaz. This was of no concern to Ahaz or Esther, as both were willing parties to and beneficiaries of all that was going on in their home. But neighbours, as neighbours often do, started to come out into the street to find out what it was that had awoken them so early on this feast day. Had Ahaz been over generous with the hospitality he'd shown to his guests? Had his guests taken advantage of him and abused his generosity by over indulging in wine and thus bringing shame on him in front of his neighbours?

The crowd in the street outside his house grew and some started to venture up the steps to look in through the door to see what was causing the commotion. "Why was there such raucous laughter and the sounds of weeping coming out of the same room? They must have been drinking!"

The collective ignorance of crowds has been seen throughout history and this crowd was no different. Suspicious of anything different, suspicious of outsiders causing trouble, they needed an explanation.

Something stirred within Peter. For a time he had become aware of noises outside their room. He had seen people brazenly standing on Ahaz's steps peering into the room, watching what was going on, but untouched by it. Just curious to know what was causing the commotion. Peter felt the need to get up and pick his way over the bodies in the room to talk to those standing in the doorway, to invite them in if they would like to join them. But he was not prepared for the sight that greeted his eyes when he got to the top step. It wasn't just a few prying neighbours poking their heads round the door to their room; there must have been hundreds of people in the street outside the house, all with their necks craned, trying to make out what was going on. As Peter stepped out he came into full view of the crowd and this elicited some finger pointing from those in the street below.

Loud comments like, "Aha! It's that lot from Galilee!"; and "Northerners always like to drink too much wine," were made so Peter could hear their condemnation.

"These Galileans never could hold their liquor," one said, and another replied, "They never know when they've had enough," which was the queue for the crowd to murmur their agreement by tutting and shaking their heads. "…and this a holy feast day too," said a priest passing by on the outer edge of the crowd, keen to join in the condemnation, but not willing to get too close to the great unwashed assembly. "What would your beloved teacher say if he could see you now? How quickly you degenerates return to you former lives of sin once your leaders are no longer with you. Go home and don't come back, you drunkards!" he spat with all the self-righteous venom he could muster.

This last comment irked Peter more than the others, not least of all because once again the religious establishment were attempting to make the truly holy work of God a profane thing, without even tasting of it themselves. It should have been no surprise to him that those who rejected the Son of God would also reject this Gift of God.

"We are not drunk as you suppose," Peter said at the top of his voice, trying to make himself heard over the noise of the crowd. The height advantage he had standing at the top of the steps helped, as did the new and unfamiliar sensation he was experiencing whist addressing the crowd. "They don't scare me!" he thought. "I am not intimidated…" he wondered and as he felt this new, unfamiliar power surge through him he decided to address the crowd further. Some jokers in the crowd were not going to let Peter get his point across without them first throwing a few more wise cracks in his direction so the rest of the crowd could see just how clever they were. But the emptiest vessels make the loudest noise and so it was evident with the loudest individuals. Peter let them finish, but held his hand up indicating that he had something to say.

Whilst this was going on James, John, Andrew and some of the other disciples had come to the door and were trying to squeeze out on to the top steps with Peter. To make room Peter had to encourage the voyeuristic neighbours to move down a couple of steps and to go back to join their families. Their indignant response to this was that they *were* with their family and Peter looked at the upturned faces below him and could see the family likenesses shared by the others who had invited themselves into Ahaz's house and climbed the steps.

"We are not drunk as you suppose," Peter repeated.

There then came more noise from inside the room as another wave of the Spirit crashed upon the disciples still lying on the floor in there. This latest wave seemed to prompt even more praise, louder than before, shouted at the tops of their voices in languages other than their own. This caused a stir in the crowd below and some, who clearly looked like pilgrims from other countries, started to shush those intent on making more wise cracks. They even asked the priest to be quiet. "Just for a moment, please!" because they could hear the wonders of God being told in their own language. With this the priest gathered his robes about him and span off down the street to find the respect he deserved from a more worthy, erudite group of people. The temple would hold such a group that he would be happier to be associated with; a type more befitting a man of his station in life, rather than this mob. He was happy to leave them. He hoped they ransacked Ahaz's house. He'd lost all faith in that man ever since he'd started associating with this lot from Galilee.

The crowd's presence outside Ahaz's house had gathered because they'd heard the unusual noises coming out of the upper room. Now they stood there and listened. Even the jokers were silenced. Each could hear as clear as a bell someone telling of the wonders of God in their own language. They could hear the message of salvation available to them through the death and resurrection of God's Son, Jesus of Nazareth, their Messiah. A hush fell over the crowd as a spirit of repentance swept over them. Peter watched from the top of the steps and was deeply moved by the scene he saw before him. He even had compassion on those impolite neighbours who seemed cut to their hearts and needed salvation as much as he or anyone did.

"This is what it looked like when Jesus worked" he thought to himself as he surveyed the crowd. "Where did this compassion that he now felt come from?"

Peter then stepped forward and addressed the crowd again, this time as the leader of the group of disciples. There was no fear. There was no hesitation. This was his calling. He knew this was going to be his life, his 'song', from now on.

Peter addressed the up-turned, hungry faces. "Fellow Jews and all of you who live in Jerusalem, let me explain this to you; listen carefully to what I say. These people are not drunk, as you suppose. It's only nine in the morning! No, this is what was spoken by the prophet Joel: 'In the last days, God says, I will pour out my Spirit on all people...'"and so Peter went on, quoting from the book of the Prophet Joel, to explain that the apparent chaos the crowd was seeing before them was God at work fulfilling that particular prophesy given by the prophet.

His first sermon was accompanied by a range of loud noises and raucous laughter that continued to emanate from the open doorway to the upper room to his immediate right. It was a little distracting for him, but gloriously so. The other disciples who came out on to the steps with him occasionally nipped back into the glorious presence inside the room, just because it was so lovely to be in there, and anyway, Peter seemed to have things under control now. As Peter concluded his address the crowd seemed genuinely moved and there was now more noise of weeping outside in the street below than there was in the upper room.

Some in the crowd started to cry out to Peter and the other disciples up there with him, "Brothers, what shall we do?" they shouted as if their lives depended on Peter's response.

Peter replied, "You must repent and be baptized, every one of you, in the name of Jesus Christ for the forgiveness of your sins. And you will receive the gift of the Holy Spirit. The promise is for you and your children and for all who are far off—for all whom the Lord our God will call."

Peter turned to his right and put his hand out to lean on the door frame. He called in through the doorway for some of the disciples by name to come out because they had work to do.

As "the noisy drunks" extricated themselves from the room, Peter continued to address the crowd, which now hung on his every word. He warned them and pleaded with them to save themselves from this corrupt generation.

Peter descended the steps and started to move out into the street, closely followed by the other disciples. Some still unsteady on their feet having just emerged from the room, looked every bit like an unruly group of drunks struggling to negotiate the steps down to the street, leaning on each other and stopping each other from falling and descending the steps face first. Once Peter was at street level all eyes remained on him and he said to the crowd, "We must go and get you baptised. Let's not wait another moment." And all those who accepted his message started to move off with him in the general direction of the valley where there was an open source of water. Thousands were baptised by him and his fellow apostles that day, from the early morning and throughout the afternoon. More believers were added to their number as passers-by witnessed the spectacle of the baptisms. When they asked what was going on they heard the message of salvation and then too received the gift of the Holy Spirit that was being poured out in the place.

Each penitent was transformed as they descended into the pool in repentance and received the sacrament of baptism. The apostles got blessed being a conduit for this gift that God was pouring out every time they baptised a new believer. The crowds pressed into the pool, eager to be baptised. The water's edge got muddied and the water became murkier as the traffic continued to pass in and out of it throughout the day.

History records that about three thousand were added to their number that day.

JUST BEFORE 3 O'CLOCK
ONE AFTERNOON

S ome weeks later at 3 o'clock one afternoon, the sun was fierce as Peter and John walked the road down the Mount of Olives back towards the Kidron Valley, as they had so many times before. Their excitement growing the nearer they got to the temple. They had been living in Jerusalem for some time now and worshipping at the temple had become a regular part of their daily routines. Their growing excitement had little to do with the magnificent edifice that it was and certainly nothing to do with the corrupt institution it housed, but everything to do with the God it was built to honour. The God that had done a transforming work in them that morning in the upper room through the gift of His Spirit. They also loved to meet up with the other believers who had been in the room at that time, sometimes just to cat with them, or socialise, but best of all was to worship with them. It was like individual glowing coals being brought together which created a white hot furnace of worship.

Apart from the various external manifest changes, internally they were all different. Each knew it, but struggled to put the change they felt into words. What they saw in each other though was a person transformed into someone who spoke more like Jesus, prayed more like Jesus and ministered more like Jesus now. Certainly more than they had ever done previously, and this change had continued unwaveringly ever since.

Communing with the other believers who had experienced this baptism of The Spirit during the Feast of Pentecost, and to be fair with those who'd subsequently received the gift, happened at a level that it could not with believers that had had no experience of this gift. There was no need to explain what they'd been thinking about or meditating on. Everyone seemed to be running in the same direction with God. More was communicated by the meeting of eyes and a shared smile than could ever easily be put into words. Each knew what the other was feeling. It was a kind of corporate, healthy infatuation with their God. Words were almost superfluous, the joy etched on each other's faces seemed indelible and was the external expression of what burned in their hearts night and day, whether they were at the temple or not. Worshipping at the temple did not scratch an itch that then went away until the following week. It was a place to meet and worship with other believers and to share the great news about Jesus, God's Messiah, with those who had either never heard of him or were yet to be convinced.

Peter, like John, and as far as he was aware most of the other believers too, had been afflicted with this insatiable desire to sneak off and be alone with God. Just to spend time alone in His presence at any point during the day or night. On reflection it was something that Jesus seemed to do a lot of, but even after being close to him for three years, Peter had not shared the same desire to do. Often finding prayer more of a chore or a discipline than a joy, an expectation that he fulfilled as a disciple rather than the high point of the day that it now seemed to be. Just as when young lovers crave each other's company when they are forced to be apart. Each filling the other's thoughts, regardless of the tasks they are obliged to work on absentmindedly, until they are able to be back in each other's arms once again. So it now was for Peter. The mundane daily tasks were things that had to be completed, had to be dispensed with, so they could no longer distract him from the one thing he knew he was made for… just to be in the presence of his God. Enjoying his God's love for him and in return being able to verbalise his own love for God. There was nothing more enjoyable, nothing quite so potent as this and it drew them all, corporately and individually, back and back again to spending time in the company of their Divine Lover.

There were other consequences of these changes that had been fashioned in them. Compassion for their neighbours was more evident, more like the compassion that Jesus showed. On top of that, so many of Jesus' teachings now seemed to make more sense where previously their meanings had eluded Peter. When asked about the greatest commandment, Jesus said, "The most important one is this: 'Hear, O Israel: The Lord our God, the Lord is one. Love the Lord your God with all your heart and with all your soul and with all your mind and with all your strength.' The second is this: 'Love your neighbour as yourself.' There is no commandment greater than these."

Loving God was something Peter had aspired to previously. If he'd said he loved God back then he would have been overstating that fact. However, now he did, without reservation, but not through any effort on his part. He just knew he did. Similarly he was endued with a compassion for those around him that he had never known before.

On another occasion Jesus had said, "If you love me, keep my commands." Well, Peter had previously struggled to keep his commands and deduced that clearly he couldn't love him very much. Not now though. Keeping Jesus' commands seemed effortless, as if because of this new love, this new infatuation. Keeping his commands was… easy… in fact the only option. There was no choice anymore; it was the only way he wanted to live from now on.

Peter and John passed between the ordered rows of olive trees either side of the road, their gnarled trunks like columns of thick, tangled rope, knotted, twisted and haphazardly piled up, their branches bowing under the weight of the valued fruit they bore. Fruit that gave the precious oil that played such a central part in life, the extraordinary product of the year's sunshine and meagre rainfall. The oil was burned in lamps to light their homes and used in temple rituals. For the mundane and the holy; for anointing priests and kings, for everyday uses like keeping leather supple and weather proof, for cooking, for pouring on wounds and to anoint the sick for healing. For some it possessed cosmetic properties to beautify when used on the hair and skin.

The olive trees were festooned with leaves alternately dark green and silver, giving the impression the trees were launching armfuls of confetti into the air in celebration, but the moment being frozen in time by the branches that held the undispersed clouds.

Beneath the trees the once green grasses that carpeted the groves were dried to a golden amber colour by the unrelenting summer sun. The trees stood silently, serenaded by the cicada's rhythmic strumming that filled the air, punctuated by the occasional shrill, high pitched trilling of small birds as they excitedly swooped to gorge on the feast of flies, which were thriving on the waste from the city's inhabitants. Lizards sunned themselves with an unmoving, static alertness on the warm trunks and low stone walls that in places retained the terraced rocky earth in curving bulwarks, holding back the weight of the hillside above them. Fig trees and pomegranates grew here and there, germinating where fruit had previously fallen. Their haphazard growth contrasting with the intentionality of the regimented rows of evenly spaced, albeit twisted and pock-marked, olive trees.

As they reached the temple Peter and John saw beggars being brought up to their usual spots at this hour. Some had already sat out all day asking for alms. Peter's first meeting with Mephibosheth had been a simple transactional one: Beggar needed money – Peter had money – Peter gave money to beggar and moved on. Beggar's need met. Peter's obligation met. Simple and unremarkable.

"Good day to you Sirs… God bless you both…" Mephibosheth started his usual patter, holding out his bowl expectantly for the men's donations. He looked familiar to Peter, but (and it was sad to admit it) so did too many of the other poor unfortunates that sat or lay along the road up to the temple. He knew he had seen this man before, as he had seen so many of them over the years, but this time he stood out from the others, as if there was some kind of light shining on him, picking him out from the rest. There was also the internal tug in Peter's chest, a fleeting, easy to miss, almost indefinable, but very definite "this one…"

Peter moved towards the man and John went with him. He responded to the man's request for money by showing him his purse and patting it as he had done before to demonstrate its emptiness. On this occasion there was absolutely nothing within the pouch, not so much as a single lepton. Mephibosheth cocked his head to one side to study its form. He listened for any sound that would indicate the presence of coins contained within it, but there was none, so he gave Peter a reluctant and disappointed look of acceptance. He turned to Peter's companion with not much expectation, only to be greeted with an apologetic smile and shake of the head with his hands held out empty, demonstrating his similar lack of funds. Done with these two, Mephibosheth started to scan his immediate environs for 'more interesting' people to engage with, but as he had no one else's attention because people seemed to speed up their walk as they drew near, glancing furtively in the opposite direction, or staring straight ahead as they scooted past, Mephibosheth started scanning further afield for more likely benefactors, Peter and John already becoming invisible to him. It was then that Peter recognised the man from their encounter earlier that year.

"Sir…" Peter said trying to regain his attention "…what is your name?"

Mephibosheth paid him no attention, focussing rather on the pressing matter of securing a few coins to buy an evening meal; starting with this next person slowly working their way towards him…

"Sir," Peter repeated, trying once more to get his attention, but Mephibosheth sat with his head strained hard to his left, waiting for the best moment to engage his unsuspecting prey as they approached. So Peter moved to his right and stood in front of him, blocking his view.

"Look at us," Peter insisted. "I don't have any silver or any gold, but what I do have I give to you…"

Mephibosheth's interest was held if only momentarily as he wondered what Peter was going to give him. He'd already said he had no money and he wasn't carrying anything, so what could he possibly…?

"…in the Name of Jesus Christ of Nazareth," Peter continued as he felt the Spirit of God flowing over him and through him, then altering his voice slightly to mimic a close approximation to Jesus' voice, he commanded the man "…walk!" It was a definite instruction that made no allowance for the apparent impossibility of the invitation.

Mephibosheth sat there stunned, looking at Peter. He wasn't stunned because he had just been confronted by a lunatic, and there were always plenty of those circulating around the crowds; but because at the moment Peter uttered the word "walk" he for the first time in his life thought he could, possibly… just maybe able to… walk. Of course he had tried through sheer determination and the encouragement of his family, but this was when he was little, but his legs just would not straighten out and the frustratingly futile attempts were short lived and embarrassing failures. Never to be repeated. Until now that is.

After 40 years of sitting on tangled legs, he now wanted to walk. Not just wanted to walk, he thought he could walk. To actually attempt the very thing most people never gave a second thought to, but had never been an option for him.

Peter bent forward and held out his left hand for Mephibosheth to take. Tentatively, excitedly, Mephibosheth reached out his right hand and took Peter's offer of help to stand up. As their hands joined, Mephibosheth felt power shoot through his arms into his chest, then down through his torso into his legs. Power was going into his powerless legs! He looked at them stunned, watching the previously useless muscles twitching in his legs as the power started to course through him. Then he looked back up into Peter's face and back down again at his legs that were still twitching, but now also started to tingle and burn as popping sounds started to emanate from his hips, knees and ankles. The noise startled him. Then gently and reassuringly Peter started to straighten up, bringing with him Mephibosheth to stand on his own two, perfectly formed, perfectly straight, perfectly matching, size nine feet.

As the world stopped turning for a moment for the two of them and fell silent about them, Mephibosheth stood looking at Peter's face, eye to eye. He then slowly bent his head and looked at the ground beneath him and his new legs and feet, which stretched all the way down to the pale stony ground he had sat on all his life. His legs! They… they… didn't look like his legs. He wiggled his toes and stared at them as they nimbly scrunched the dirt between them. He looked back at Peter, then back down at his feet again, wiggled his toes some more, then looked up into Peter's smiling face again. Mephibosheth smiled too. Peter took half a step back whilst holding on to Mephibosheth's hand and Mephibosheth took his first step away from his mat, following Peter's lead, like a man stepping out on to a high mountain ledge, or over a terrifyingly deep ravine. Peter smiled and took another step backwards and Mephibosheth followed him, still holding his hand. Peter took another step backwards, like a parent would, encouraging his child to take their first steps, and so

Mephibosheth started to walk.

The world started turning again and noise started to break into their consciousness once more. John looked at Peter trying to catch his eye, to mouth something to his friend, but Peter was transfixed by the man before him.

Passers-by stopped passing by, slowed and stopped, staring openmouthed at what they were seeing. John included.

New arrivals asked, "What's going on? What has happened?"

A beautiful pastel blue butterfly flitted and wove its way between the gawping statues and settled on some wild flowers growing out of the top of a crumbling wall nearby. The only one of God's creatures in the immediate vicinity seemingly unaffected by the unfolding events.

After a few more steps, the two men stopped their slow waltz. Peter asked, "Do you think you can walk by yourself now?" Mephibosheth wasn't sure, but thought he could. So with his right hand Peter removed Mephibosheth's vice-like grip on the hand he had first offered him. Mephibosheth looked over his shoulder at his mat where he had been sitting, which was now some ten metres behind him, and stared at it for a moment, before turning back to look at Peter. "Wha' di' you do…?"

Mephibosheth was still clutching his grubby, cracked little begging bowl in his left hand which was hanging limply by his side. Peter reached down and said, "I don't think you'll need this anymore," and with that he took the small bowl from Mephibosheth and tossed it back towards his mat. Mephibosheth turned and watched it bounce once with a hollow pop, break into two fragments which spun out of sight, landing somewhere behind the mat. Then in answer to Mephibosheth's question Peter said, "God has healed you… in the name of Jesus Christ of Nazareth. I did nothing." Peter raised his voice and repeated the sentence as he became aware of the crowd that were starting to gather around them, keen that no one should credit him with the miracle.

"Wha…?" Mephibosheth's face was a picture of incomprehension "Wha...?" he repeated. "Nazareth…?" he asked seeking clarity on a point of detail that really didn't explain what had just happened. Nothing was making sense to him. His world had just changed.

"You are healed," said Peter smiling.

Mephibosheth smiled back. He then smiled some more. He smiled at those looking on and they smiled back. He looked at John. John was already smiling and Mephibosheth smiled at him too. That made John laugh, which made Mephibosheth laugh and he embraced Peter, who had started laughing, too. John joined the pair of them and the three of them embraced. They then did a series of little jumps together in a small circle. Mephibosheth had never jumped before, but he was about to do a lot of jumping very soon because it felt good to jump. Exceedingly good. He would not be able to refrain from jumping as his excitement grew.

He turned his face to the sky and started praising God at the top of his voice. At the top of his voice. He was quite loud and unreserved about it. He let go of Peter and John and thrusting the palms of his hands towards heaven, started shouting his thanks and praise to God, turning on the spot where he stood.

After an appropriately long period of thanksgiving, because it is never good to interrupt someone's genuine selfless praise and thanks to God, Peter tapped Mephibosheth on the shoulder and said to him, "You know… it's customary around these parts to worship God *in* His temple, not just standing outside." Peter emphasised the word "in" and pointed to the Beautiful Gate just in front of them.

Mephibosheth stopped momentarily to look at Peter and take in what he had just said. Peter nodded and moved his eyes towards the gate for Mephibosheth to follow his gaze.

"In there…?" Mephibosheth asked almost conspiratorially, seeking confirmation that he would be allowed in after a lifetime's exclusion due to his "curse".

"Yes," said Peter reassuringly, putting his arm around the man, indicating for John to do likewise on the other side. The three of them moved slowly up the steps and in through the gate. Mephibosheth's legs did not need their support, but his emotions did.

Once inside Mephibosheth freed himself from the men's embrace and started to circle around, taking in his new surroundings with his arms outstretched. His God had been waiting for him for forty years, longing for men to allow this son of Israel into His courts, where he would always have been welcome, with or without tangled legs.

Without any sense of self-consciousness Mephibosheth started his heartfelt praising and worshipping of God again, oblivious to any protocol. He started with a few tentative steps, describing a wide circle around Peter and John. Then as he realised his legs were perfectly strong enough, he started running whilst praising, again shouting at the top of his voice, startling a few nearby who weren't used to this kind of thing. They gave him some old fashioned disapproving looks, but God didn't. He loved it! Others did too. There were always some who wanted to worship freely, but seldom had the excuse to do so, but now they did and they started to follow Mephibosheth's lead and joined with his unbridled joy, thanking God for the miracle they were witnessing; for they knew this man who used to sit outside and beg. They had seen him many, many times before today.

Mephibosheth slalomed in and out of Solomon's Colonnade with childlike joy, adding jumps and skips as he went, going through the full repertoire of the varied permutations of movement God had endowed his legs with. Others followed suit behind him snaking in and out of the pillars, rejoicing in their God, who had shown compassion on their fellow Israelite. Peter and John stood laughing as they watched the man's undignified, unfettered joy and sensing God's delight in what was unfolding and the worship it brought. They clapped along to the extravagant, if a little ungainly, dance which Mephibosheth was leading.

The commotion started to draw the attention of those around the temple and more people started to run to where the three men were. Well, actually where Peter, John and a long meandering procession were, with Mephibosheth at the head. And because the gathering crowd wanted to know what had happened to trigger all this, Peter started to explain as best he could how this man at the front of the mayhem had been crippled from birth, but had just been healed by faith in the name of Jesus. This last bit caused a ripple of excitement among some and resentment among others. They knew of Jesus and what had been done to him, because of the way he had challenged the system, and this… this started to look a bit like the scenes they'd witnessed when Jesus would have been the one teaching here. But instead of it being the man Jesus himself, it would appear that two of his followers seemed to have picked up his mantle and were carrying on the same sort of wonders "in his name", as it were, as if the Galilean himself was still there. Still alive.

It didn't take long for the Chief Priests and temple authorities to stamp out the joy before it could spread. They especially didn't like that Galilean's name brought up in public again. They'd gone to great lengths to get rid of him, so the captain of the temple guard, with some priests under the orders of the Sadducees, approached Peter and John with the intent of arresting them to throw them in jail for the night. Although Malchus was once again despatched with this arresting party, he directed operations from the rear of the group this time, making sure he was safely out of reach of that big fisherman. He made sure Peter was securely tied and relieved of any weapons, which he might have been carrying. No one in the arresting party was actually listening to Malchus's instructions, but just got on with the task in hand. The whiney, irritating voice continued to chirrup away from behind the biggest and fiercest looking of the temple guards, regardless.

The binding of Peter and John did not dampen their spirits, but it did put a stop to the worship and dancing, led by Mephibosheth, who in all his innocence looked on in utter confusion at the authority's reaction to the celebrating. Why would they do that? he asked himself, then others around him. No one wanted to get into that debate now and a couple of those who had been dancing closest to Mephibosheth and were breathing quite heavily took him by the arm and led him back out of the gate he'd come through, reassuring him by saying, "That was a wonderful time. Thank you brother. Maybe we should leave it there for today, and perhaps resume this tomorrow?"

Peter and John were promptly lead away, but both were straining their necks trying to see where Mephibosheth was, hoping he was alright. The fact that he hadn't been tied up with them meant he probably was.

For the first time in his life Mephibosheth walked home from the temple that day. It was at an hour just before his brothers would normally come to fetch him, loading him on to the old hand cart and dragging him through the narrow allies back to their small house, which was sited just inside the wall to the west of the city. On the back of the cart he would be bounced down the endless stone steps and dragging up others that lay between the house and the temple where he begged each day. Before he left the temple he picked up his old mat, rolled it up and tucked it under his left arm. As he headed home, various scenarios ran through his mind as he pictured his family's reaction to his transformation. A lot of the people he would normally greet from the back of the hand cart didn't even glance at him, presuming him a stranger. To be fair he felt like a king today and probably exuded an unfamiliar and dignified air as he walked. He would have stopped to explain what had happened to the people he knew, but he had to tell his family first, and the excitement grew as he neared home and as he thought about how it was going to pan out.

He was a little over half way back when he recognised the sound of their creaky old cart being bounced down some steps less than fifty metres ahead of where he stood. It was the younger of his two brothers, Eli, who had that fed up, annoyed expression he always had when he had to collect Mephibosheth by himself. The older brother had on this occasion made himself scarce when it was time for the collection.

"Eli!" he called out, smiling and waving his free hand to attract his brother's attention above the throng of people that were crowded around the stalls in the narrow bazaar.

"Eli!" he called again. His brother not twenty metres away now.

Eli looked up, but only momentarily as he had to negotiate his way around people without bumping into them or crushing exposed toes under the heavy wheels of his cart, worn elliptical through years of use up and down these stone steps. He slowed his progress so he could glance up again at the man calling his name. He looked at Mephibosheth with a puzzled expression on his face. The voice sounded like his brother's, but obviously wasn't. He came closer, emerging from the thicket of people into the clearing just in front of his brother. Eli stopped, looked at his brother and dropped the cart handles, which clattered on the smooth stone surface. Mephibosheth put out his (new) left foot to stop the cart from continuing its journey down the steep slope unpiloted. He wanted to embrace his brother who had still not said anything, so he wedged his mat under one of the wheels, and stood up straight, smiling at his brother eye to eye, for the first time. Tears filled his brother's eyes as he shook his head, unable to comprehend what stood before him. The two brothers embraced.

"What has happened to you...?" his brother asked into Mephibosheth's ear as they clung to each other. It was the only question to ask. He pulled back and held his older brother at arm's length to look at him again. Well to be specific, to look at his brother's legs and feet. Mephibosheth told him breathlessly and in a somewhat muddled order what had happened to him, interspersing it frequently with "Hallelujahs" and "Isn't it amazing!" and "God be praised!" and so on. Their encounter had passed largely unobserved by those buying goods in the bazaar, only turning round occasionally when Mephibosheth couldn't contain his joy and he started shouting heavenwards again.

Very quickly the two headed for home. Taking a handle each, they shared the chore of dragging the hand cart back up the smooth steps it had just been bounced down. Eli kept glancing at his brother, laughing and shaking his head. From time to time he'd check if he was okay. Did he want to rest? Does he need to ride the rest of the way?

Mephibosheth reassured him he had never felt better. He didn't need to rest and if Eli was tired he could hop on the cart himself and ride the rest of the way home. They laughed, but Eli was not going to let his brother strain himself unnecessarily in case it undid the good that had just been done, not sure how permanent the transformation was.

When they got to their house, their old mother was sat with her back to the door, stirring a blackened cooking pot balanced on top of a small brazier.

Without turning around she said, "Eli, could you put your brother round the back with his father for now? I have some clearing up to do in here before we can eat. Leave him there until it's time to eat."

When she had finished giving her instructions, without taking her eye off the pot that was coming to the boil, Mephibosheth put his arms around his mother and hugged her.

Still watching the pot, she patted his arm and thinking it was Eli, said "Bless you my son, but could you please take your brother out the back? I have a lot to do."

"Mother… it's me," Mephibosheth whispered in her ear.

"What...? Who...?"

"It's me, mother," he said, rephrasing the statement.

She turned on her low stool to look at him. Then she turned some more to get a proper look, shrieked, fainted and fell off the stool, narrowly missing the brazier and their evening meal.

"Mother!" Mephibosheth called out for fear he'd killed her. "Mother, are you alright…?

"Eli… !"

"I'm right behind you brother." Their mother lay on her back and moaned weakly. "I think she'll be alright," Eli said as he stepped around his brother and dipped a cloth in the pitcher of water and wiped his mother's forehead. She started to revive and looked at Mephibosheth. Then she wailed and passed out again.

Eventually after some time she was able to sit back on the stool, take her first born son's face in her hands to reassure herself that this vision before her was indeed Mephibosheth, then smothered him with her kisses and her tears. This went on for quite some time, so Eli went to the rear of the house to find his father. The white-bearded old man wanted to know what the commotion was and when their meal would be ready. Eli told him he had better come inside and see.

"Is the meal ready? I can't smell bread yet? Are we not having bread tonight? Tell me son, why are we not having bread? Why did your mother scream?"

"Just come inside father," Eli said as he helped his father to his feet and gently guided the old man around the side of the house to the doorway, all the time accompanied by the sound of the mother's commotion coming from within. Eli drew back the drape covering the doorway, holding it to one side. With a sideways motion of his head he indicated that his father should go inside. His father's eyesight was poor and it took some time for his rheumy eyes to adjust to the dark interior. He could hear his wife crying, gesturing at the tall stranger standing before him.

"Who are you?" he asked, then turning to Eli he said, "You didn't say we had a guest for dinner tonight."

"Father it is I… Mephibosheth. I… I have been healed. Look, I can stand. I can walk…"

The father's trembling hands trembled all the more as he failed to understand what was being said and who it was telling him these things. Mephibosheth drew nearer to his father so the old man could see him better.

"Father, it is me." He said it more tenderly this time and the old man stretched out a crooked hand and touched his son's face and then hair. He touched his shoulder and looked him up and down. His watery old eyes filled up and large tears rolled down his weathered cheekbones and into his thin white beard.

"God is merciful," he said at last, as much to himself as to those around him, remembering the old woman's words on the night of his son's birth, then sat down, unable to comprehend the act of grace that had been shown to his family.

The next morning Mephibosheth was keen to resume his worship at the temple and headed off early as the land was still bracing itself to endure the heat of the coming day. This time he was accompanied by both brothers, but no hand cart. Sadly, his arrival had been expected and he was picked up by the temple guard and immediately brought before the Council of the Sanhedrin, which had been convened to try Peter and John. Ironically his very presence in the chamber served as supporting material evidence for the defence of Peter and John, rather than giving weight for the prosecution, as the captain of the guard thought he might;

perceiving him as just another antagonist upsetting the status quo.

Peter and John were acquitted, more out of the Council's fear of the reaction of the large number of people who were supportive of this fledgling band of believers, than out of any real sense of justice. But before they were let go they were threatened not to speak in the name of this Jesus anymore. Somewhat bravely, neither Peter nor John were prepared to agree to these terms, but knew all too well the severe consequences they faced if they did not adhere to them. They were after all now standing before the same men that had recently brought about the death of Jesus.

The pair discussed what they should do as they walked back to the house of Ahaz, which had been offered to them indefinitely as their home for as long as they wanted to stay in the city. Ahaz, Esther and their family being more than happy to be the group's hosts. Peter and John thought it only right that they explain to everyone based at the house that they had attracted the attention of the religious ruling parties, much as Jesus had done, and as a consequence they were potentially liable for similar treatment if they continued to teach and minister in his name.

This opposition to teaching 'in the name of Jesus' started that day in the Sanhedrin, but continued for centuries to come. Being religious, spiritual, or godly, or even a 'tentative theist' is acceptable, but mention the name of Jesus Christ and people are immediately divided. Being spiritual is all well and good and can make someone a better person, so long as they keep it to themselves, but bring Jesus into the equation and hackles will get raised.

Peter and John were not going to put any proposals to the group to vote on. It was clear to both of them what must continue to be done, as confirmed by God's healing of Mephibosheth, but people should be given the option of staying within the group and facing the potential cost of doing so, or backing out if the personal cost or risk of punishment was too much for them. They would then pray, laying it all before God and seek his empowering to be bolder, more effective witnesses for Him. And this is what they did.

No one left the group that day. This response by the Sanhedrin had always been expected; it had just been verbalised today.

The group gathered in the upper room and prayed together, as they often did. This time they acknowledged their weakness before God and sought an increased boldness from Him to complete the work they knew He had for them to do. The stones and timber of the room started to shake again, as it had the first time the Spirit fell on them during Pentecost. Small rivulets of dust bled from joints between timber and masonry. Dirt and granules of dust drifted down from the roof materials above them. Now the Holy Spirit fell on them again as he had done before, but in a different way this time. There was still the awe and wonder of God. There was the weight of his Glory in the room. Spontaneous worship erupted in their own tongues and unknown languages. There was an energy passing through each of them and each shook and trembled violently under the action of God's Spirit moving on human flesh. He melted fears away and as the fears melted He replaced them with such a sense of wonder and love for Him that an iron will formed, an immoveable divine determination to be his witnesses, irrespective of personal cost. Much as Jesus had been seen to manifest. Always seeking God's guidance and glorification above anything else; in everything He did. The meeting was timeless and continued until God had completed the work he needed to complete in these young Apostles.

The Apostles' message of salvation spread, accompanied by signs and wonders like the one worked in the former beggar Mephibosheth, but also the less spectacular miracles such as the healings of short term disorders like fevers, headaches and injuries. Each act displaying God's love for the individual and his invitation for them to get to know him through his one and only Son, Jesus Christ. This gospel was preached and put into practice in this way, by men and women mimicking their Lord's way of ministering, showing other men and women how to do the same works. Men and women who carried the message without wilting in the face of the fierce heat of the murderous persecution that broke out against them. They seeded the fertile soil of the communities they lived in with the ways and truths of messiah Jesus. Their message swept throughout the extent of their known world and beyond, eventually encompassing all peoples of the Earth.

EPILOGUE

Peter and the other Apostles that Jesus chose (with the exception of Judas Iscariot) gave their lives to spreading the message of salvation through Jesus Christ and continuing to work miracles, in his name. It is held that all bar John were executed for their efforts. Peter's days being ended in Rome sometime between AD64 and AD68. Tradition has it that he was crucified upside down. This inverted position on the executioners' cruel apparatus was apparently at his own request, deeming himself unworthy to be crucified in the same manner as his beloved Saviour. The simple fisherman from his humble home in Capernaum. An impulsive man, prone to misunderstandings, ashamed of the fear he showed and succumbed to on the night that Jesus was arrested, but never denying him again. Victorious over his fears in the most terrifying arena and very public spectacle of his execution, in the capital city of the world's superpower of his day. He showed no man could intimidate him. No man would ever again make him deny his Lord and Saviour who he loved, *more than all the others*, more than life itself. This final act, as the soldiers set about their task of crucifying him, was an extravagant act of worship if you will; undoubtedly an impetuous one, requesting to be crucified differently to his Lord. Peter would have known his Saviour looked on, watching over him, as the cruel nails were driven through his wrists into the wood of the cross beam and shattering his heel bones as they pinned his body to the wooden upright. Peter poured himself out one last time for his Lord.

In his last moments as they hoisted him into position and the nails took the full weight of his body as it slumped head down, his gasps would have delighted the jeering crowd gathered to watch his agonies, humiliation and eventually his death. But the victory was his, not theirs. He would have known the eyes of his friend and Saviour were upon him, ready and eager to receive him into glory, to embrace once more his impulsive, spontaneous, hot-headed, reckless-to-the-end, but faithful-to-the-end; fearless and deeply loved friend.

His eyes flickered and closed one last time. Peter's song, the song he had only ever wanted to sing for his Lord, concluded with a sigh as his final breath left his body.